"Self-compassion is a powerful resource for coping with whatever life sends our way. When adults learn it, they often say, 'Why didn't I learn this sooner?' Well, now we can start to learn at the earliest possible age. This superb workbook captures the depth and scope of self-compassion in simple, totally delightful practices and activities. Highly recommended for parents, teachers, therapists, and anyone who loves kids."

—**Christopher Germer, PhD**, lecturer on psychiatry at Harvard Medical School, codeveloper of the Mindful Self-Compassion program, and author of *The Mindful Path to Self-Compassion*

"As both a parent and teacher, this workbook by Hobbs and Balentine, *The Self-Compassion Workbook for Kids*, is my new go-to for teaching, sharing, and supporting kids in learning self-compassion. It's packed full of so many fun, engaging, and supporting practices that are not only essential to help kids, but also an excellent resource for anyone who teaches, parents, and supports the children of our world. This practical and accessible guide will truly change how we can bring the practices of self-compassion to kids."

—**Lisa Baylis, MEd**, teacher, counselor, and author of *Self-Compassion for Educators*

"Hobbs and Balentine have crafted an engaging psychoeducational workbook on self-compassion for youth. The book expertly scaffolds readers from breathing exercises to emotion regulation and values exploration, and includes cleverly linked audio tracks, written mindfulness exercises, yoga, craft activities, and fun educational challenges. It invites children to learn about kindness, compassion, and mindfulness through workbook tasks and added practices. As a child psychologist and author, I highly recommend it!"

—**Amy R. Murrell, PhD**, licensed psychologist; coauthor of *The Joy of Parenting*; and author of The Becca Epps Series about Bending Your Thoughts, Feelings, and Behaviors

"Lorraine and Amy have created a treasure trove of practices that will help children and their grown-ups cultivate kindness and compassion inside themselves and in the world around them."

—**Christopher Willard, PsyD**, faculty at Harvard Medical School, and coauthor of *Alphabreaths*

"Lorraine Hobbs and Amy Balentine's *The Self-Compassion Workbook for Kids* is remarkable in its simplicity and usefulness. Its lovely, accessible format gives kids and their caregivers a step-by-step approach to experiencing self-compassion directly, and becoming their own best friend. Highly recommended."

—**Susan Kaiser Greenland**, author of *The Mindful Child, Mindful Games,* and The Inner Kids Program

"Full of creative and engaging exercises, this gem of a book guides children in developing and practicing the self-compassion that allows us to flourish."

—**Tara Brach**, author of *Radical Acceptance and Trusting the Gold*

"Dear Kids, this lovely book takes you on a journey to discover your inner superpower of kindness and mindfulness. You'll have fun, play games, make crafts, enjoy nature, and learn how to tame your inner dragon and make friends with your inner bully all at the same time!"

—**Dzung X. Vo, MD**, author of *The Mindful Teen*

"This book is a fabulous resource for children, parents, teachers, and grandparents. The authors make self-compassion accessible and fun, which is no small feat. Packed with creative games and activities, it is both practical and delightful. In fact, it is good for children of all ages!"

—**Susan M. Pollak, EdD**, cofounder of the Center for Mindfulness and Compassion at Harvard Medical School, and author of *Self-Compassion for Parents*

"If you are a parent, grandparent, or work with children, I strongly recommend you pick up this book and keep it handy. Full of practical exercises you can use today, it is a beautiful and accessible handbook for helping kids develop the lifelong healthy habit of self-compassion, which we now know is a key building block of psychological resilience and well-being. As a bonus, when you practice *with* kids, you are sure to benefit as well."

—**Cassandra Vieten, PhD**, executive director of the John W. Brick Mental Health Foundation; acting director of the Center for Mindfulness at the University of California, San Diego; and author of *Mindful Motherhood*

The Self-Compassion Workbook for Kids

Fun Mindfulness Activities to Build Emotional Strength & Make Kindness Your Superpower

Lorraine M. Hobbs, MA • Amy C. Balentine, PhD

Instant Help Books
An Imprint of New Harbinger Publications, Inc.

Publisher's Note

This publication is designed to provide accurate and authoritative information in regard to the subject matter covered. It is sold with the understanding that the publisher is not engaged in rendering psychological, financial, legal, or other professional services. If expert assistance or counseling is needed, the services of a competent professional should be sought.

Distributed in Canada by Raincoast Books

Copyright © 2023 by Lorraine M. Hobbs and Amy C. Balentine
Instant Help Books
An imprint of New Harbinger Publications, Inc.
5674 Shattuck Avenue
Oakland, CA 94609
www.newharbinger.com

FSC
www.fsc.org
MIX
Paper from responsible sources
FSC® C011935

The Self-Compassion Workbook for Kids is adapted from the Mindful Self-Compassion Program for Teens (formerly Making Friend with Yourself), co-developed by Lorraine Hobbs and Karen Bluth. The original content is based on the Mindful Self-Compassion Program created by Chris Germer and Kristin Neff, who generously granted permission to use the adapted material for this workbook.

The poem "Who is In Your Box of Crayons" is from The Crayon Box That Talked (Scholastic 1998) and is copyright © Shane Derolf. Used by permission.

The meditation "A Kid Just Like Me" is adapted from Chade Meng-Tan's "A Person Just Like Me" from The Search Inside Myself copyright © HarperCollins 2012. Used by permission.

Cover design and illustration by Sara Christian. Interior book design by Amy Shoup.
Acquired by Tesilya Hanauer. Edited by Brady Kahn.

Library of Congress Cataloging-in-Publication Data on file

Printed in the United States of America

25   24   23

10   9   8   7   6   5   4   3   2   1   First Printing

We dedicate this workbook to our
own children and all those children
we had the pleasure of learning from
throughout the years who helped
inspire the creation of this book.

Contents

Chapter 3: Growing Kindness

Chapter 4: Compassion Is Your Superpower

Chapter 5: Your Inner Bully Meets Your Superhero

Chapter 6: What Matters Most to You

Chapter 7: How to Tame Your Inner Dragon

Chapter 8: Gratitude Makes You Happy

Foreword

In this delightful and fun-filled workbook, kids can learn how to deeply care for themselves and to manage stress in a world that is rapidly changing. Unfortunately, kids in general are experiencing higher rates of distress than ever before, leading to a national emergency in mental health for children and youth. This is happening at a time when kids should be immersed in critical stages of learning.

Whether they are facing trauma because of abuse, significant losses, everyday anxiety about the pandemic, or peer pressure, kids need even more support now at a time when we are facing significant shortages in mental health resources.

This is why self-compassion is such a valuable tool for young people; self-compassion means being a good friend to yourself when you are struggling. It is an opportunity for kids to make compassion a superpower that can help with some of the scary and uncomfortable parts of being young. Ask any kid about the bullies at school or the pressures of social media!

Research shows that self-compassion can reduce anxiety, worry, and stress in teens when they learn to practice self-care, and it also reduces suicidal ideation. Studies also indicate that kids are happier, thrive, and function better when they build the emotional resources through self-compassion that help them face life difficulties. Mindfulness helps kids to focus their attention in the here and now and has the potential to quiet the mind and reduce negative thoughts and emotions. Self-compassion focuses on warmth so that kids can be kind, supportive, and accepting of themselves. This warmth, plus the mindful awareness, has the capacity to help kids deal with the tough stuff in life and reach their full potential. Research shows that the encouragement and constructive criticism through the lens of self-compassion are more effective motivators than harsh self-judgment, helping kids to develop a growth orientation and learn from failure as a part of life.

The powerful practices offered in this workbook can help kids build emotional strength and resilience, especially in times of distress. Kids can learn many wonderful meditations and activities that are age appropriate and drawn largely from the Mindful Self-Compassion for Teens program (MSC-T), an adaptation of the adult Mindful Self-Compassion (MSC) program created by my colleague Chris Germer and myself.

There is no doubt that kids will benefit from the teachings in this workbook. It is an invaluable resource for teachers, parents, pediatricians, and other professionals who work with children. Every child and every parent should have this workbook in their library and every classroom would benefit from integrating these practices into their curriculum.

Kristin Neff, PhD

A Letter to Parents and Professionals

This workbook was created to give parents, caregivers, therapists, and teachers an accessible, engaging way to introduce the skills of mindfulness and self-compassion to elementary school-aged children. While each activity can be pulled from the workbook and stand alone, the richest experience will come in taking children through the workbook from beginning to end. This will allow them to develop some basic skills in mindfulness and self-compassion at the beginning of the workbook before tackling more challenging subjects and meditations that require a little more practice and skill, found later in the workbook, such as taming the dragon of big emotions.

The workbook is based on a six-week, online mindful self-compassion program for kids and their caregivers, A Friend in Me, which we created. This program introduces children to mindfulness and self-compassion and develops their ability to befriend themselves and others, even in difficult times and challenging circumstances. This program is adapted from the teen program Mindful Self-Compassion for Teens, the only authorized adaptation from the adult Mindful Self-Compassion program, created by Chris Germer and Kristin Neff.

Because mindfulness is a practice that brings us into the present moment, we wanted the workbook activities to invite the hearts and minds of children into a felt sense of their present moment experience. Therefore, we included fun and engaging activities that can take place outside the workbook, including yoga poses, crafts, and outdoor activities to invite children to awaken their senses and connect with the world around them.

We invite the adults that use this workbook with children to engage fully with them in the activities. Several of the activities are ideally completed with another person. We learn in relationship and community, so there is nothing so inspiring for a child than to see an adult learning along with them, modeling the skills as well as valuing them. This also gives children a chance to see that they are not alone in the challenges they face and the big emotions they feel. Struggle is a shared human experience and it helps children to treat themselves with kindness when they see that they are not the only ones in need of compassion.

From time to time, activities will need adult supervision and guidance for safety, such as using scissors or going for a walk. These are noted in the workbook.

We realize children are differently abled. If you come to activities that aren't suited to your child, make adjustments so they can enjoy them in their own way. Meet children where they are, listening to how they are responding to the activities. And remember that mindfulness is a *practice*. These activities are designed to help children develop their awareness muscle so they can recognize when they are struggling and turn toward themselves with kindness and compassion. Children will continue to grow and develop their practice in their own time.

We invite you to go through the practices and workbook activities with a light touch. Hopefully, this is just the beginning of their mindfulness journey, so join us in making the workbook an accessible and fun-filled opportunity to get started on this path.

Warmly,

Lorraine Hobbs, MA

Amy Balentine, PhD

A Letter to Kids

Dear Kids,

We are so glad that you are trying out activities in this workbook that make it easier to be a good friend to yourself. We want all kids to know that we all have big emotions and tough times and sometimes feel like giving up or losing it. Through the activities, art, crafts, and meditations in this workbook, you will learn to treat yourself and others with kindness. And you will learn to pay attention to yourself and the world around you in a new way. This will help you work through hard times by encouraging and calming yourself instead of being really hard on yourself or others.

We invite you to give everything in the workbook a try. In addition to the activities in this workbook, some helpful audio tracks are available at http://www.newharbinger.com/50645. Here, you can also find printable templates to help you make fun crafts and games.

Act as if you have never done anything like this before. Be curious. When we give things a real chance, they can sometimes surprise us. When you're really curious about something you are interested in, you take the time to investigate it. That is the secret of mindfulness.

May you make kindness your superpower and find a good friend in yourself!

Lorraine and Amy

CHAPTER 1

Learning to Be Kind to Yourself

Have you ever noticed when someone you care about is injured that you really want to help them? For example, you might ask them if they're okay or you might get them help. When you want to help someone in need, you are showing compassion and being a friend. Compassion is something that everyone needs, including you. Everyone has difficult moments in life and can get their feelings hurt when someone says or does something unkind.

Did you also know that you can be a good friend to yourself in the same way you are to others? In this chapter, you will learn how to take care of yourself when you need it the most. This is called *self-compassion*, which is like putting on a warm jacket or getting a hug from someone you love. The great thing about self-compassion is that it is always there for you, and you don't have to earn it or compete for it. It is like a friend who motivates you to do your best and, when you fail, picks you up to help keep you going.

"Could I Use Some Self-Compassion?"

As you're learning to become a friend to yourself, here is an opportunity to see how much self-compassion you already give yourself. **Please circle the answers that describe you the best.**

1. **When I fail at something, I usually:**

   a. Try again

   b. Give up

   c. Cry or get angry and yell

2. **When something bad happens to me, I usually:**

   a. Talk to someone who understands

   b. Feel all alone or feel bad about myself

   c. Blame others

3. **When someone is unkind to me, I usually:**

   a. Do something soothing and kind to make myself feel better, like listening to music

   b. Say mean things or criticize myself

   c. Say mean things to them and try to get back at them

4. **When I feel afraid to talk to others, I usually:**

   a. Try to encourage myself

   b. Shy away and avoid them

   c. Act like I don't care about them

5. **When I'm in a challenging situation, I usually:**

   a. Take a few deep breaths to relax myself

   b. Back out or feel too sick to go on

   c. Fail on purpose

6. **When I compare myself to others, I usually:**

   a. See how we all have a hard time sometimes

   b. Don't think I'm good enough

   c. Put others down

Can you guess which answers are examples of self-compassion? If you guessed it's the "a" answers, you are right. You may have circled a few of these. The "b" and "c" answers are common ways that kids handle difficulty. No matter what you circled, this workbook will give you some great tools to help you handle struggles and big emotions and learn how to be kind to yourself.

So now, you can begin your journey by learning to breathe with kindness.

Rainbow Breathing

Rainbow Breathing is a way to care for yourself and a great way to start your self-compassion journey. As you focus on your breath, you may notice how your mind and body naturally settle and become calm.

This practice focuses on breathing while you paint the colors of the rainbow into the sky and into the earth. Stand with your feet hip-width apart and planted firmly on the ground and your arms by your sides and your palms turned out.

1. Imagine all the colors of the rainbow spread across the fingertips of both hands.

2. As you inhale, raise your arms up toward the sky, painting the sky with the colors of the rainbow.

3. Bring your arms all the way over your head and then turn your palms out and lower your arms as you exhale, bringing the colors of the rainbow down into the earth and into your heart.

4. Repeat this three times, inhaling, exhaling, and painting the sky.

Next you will learn another way to calm yourself while sitting at your desk.

Follow the Rainbow

First, color in each arc of the rainbow with a different color of your choice.

Then, trace each color with your finger, starting with the up arrow as you breathe in. Then, as you breathe out, move your finger around the rainbow to the down arrow. Trace each of the colors, inhaling and exhaling to help calm you.

How Can You Be a Friend to Yourself?

Now, take some time to learn more about how to be a good friend to yourself. **Choose a situation from this list and circle it:**

- Your friend didn't get invited to a party.

- Your friend didn't get on a sports team.

- Your friend got into trouble at school.

- Your friend failed a test.

- Your friend got left out and was sitting alone at lunch.

Close your eyes and think about what actions you could take to show your friend kindness if this happened to them. Write down what you could say. **Write down what you could do to comfort them.**

MORE

Now, close your eyes and think about how you might treat yourself if this happened to you. **Then, write down in the speech bubble what you would say to yourself or how you would treat yourself.**

What if we could be as kind and gentle with ourselves as we are with our friends and family when things go wrong? This is what self-compassion is all about— learning to be kind and gentle with ourselves.

Soothing Touch

When you offer yourself a kind and soothing touch, your brain and body know how to work together to comfort you. Now you can try out different ways to care for yourself with soothing touch. **See if you can feel the kindness with each soothing touch:**

- Slowly rubbing your hands together

- Placing one or two hands on your cheek

- Crossing your arms and giving a gentle hug or squeeze

- Placing one or two hands over your heart

- Placing one hand on your belly

- Placing one hand on your belly and one over your heart

- Getting a hug from your mom, dad, or your caregiver

- Squeezing your hands together

Now that you have tried these ways to soothe yourself, **write down which ones were your favorite** and try to soothe yourself these ways when you need it. Or you may have your own way that's different from anything on this list. That's fine too.

_____

_____

_____

You can download an audio track of this practice at http://www.newharbinger.com/50645.

ACTIVITY 6

Three Steps to Self-Compassion

Here are three easy steps to help you on your way to becoming a good friend to yourself, especially in difficult moments.

Step 1: Pay attention. Paying attention to how you are in the moment helps you know when you're having a hard time. Write down an example of when you were having a hard time, like when you got a bad grade or when someone was mean to you or you felt left out.

_____

_____

Step 2: Be kind to yourself. Self-kindness means treating yourself like you would treat a good friend, like giving yourself what you need to feel better. How do you usually take care of yourself? What do you do to help yourself feel better? Get a hug from your mom, pet your dog, go to your room to lie down and hug your favorite pillow. Write down what you do to take care of yourself:

_____

_____

_____

Step 3: Remember you're not alone. You're not alone in feeling bad. All kids feel alone and have hard times. It's one of the things kids and all human beings have in common. **Write down one or two people who can remind you that you are not alone.**

Use the decoder below to change the numbers into letters and discover some kind words just for you:

Decoder:

A	B	C	D	E	F	G	H	I	J	K	L	M
1	2	3	4	5	6	7	8	9	10	11	12	13

N	O	P	Q	R	S	T	U	V	W	X	Y	Z
14	15	16	17	18	19	20	21	22	23	24	25	26

Message for you:

3-15-13-16-1-19-19-9-15-14   2-5-7-9-14-19

23-9-20-8   13-5

Check your answer at the bottom of the page.

The next activity builds strength in caring for yourself when you are feeling big emotions.

Decoder message: Compassion begins with me.

Cat/Cow Yoga Pose

Stretching your spine like animals do when they wake up from a nap can make you more flexible. It's also a fun way to care for yourself and stretch out tightness or stress. This pose can help to calm your mind and body and help to focus your attention. Give it a try.

1. Come to your hands and knees on the floor (or you can use a yoga mat).

2. Spread your fingers wide to support yourself.

3. Check that your shoulders and elbows are directly over your hands and that your hips are directly over your knees.

4. Make you back flat, like a tabletop.

COW POSE

CAT POSE

5. Inhale, look up toward the ceiling, and let your belly button drop toward the floor.

6. Exhale, gently drop your head, and lift your belly button up toward your spine as you round your back.

7. Repeat three to five times, moving your belly up and down as you breathe.

8. To finish, inhale and make your back flat like a tabletop.

Next do the Child's pose.

MORE

1. From the previous position, bring your tailbone and hips down toward your heels, toes facing behind you.

2. Stretch your arms forward and place your forehead on the floor.

3. After a few breaths, bring your arms and hands next to your feet.

4. Rest here for a few gentle breaths, feeling the same powerful stillness all animals feel after they stretch their spine.

Child's pose helps you rest and digest and slows down your heart rate.

Breathing is something that is happening all the time, even when you are not paying attention. Your body just knows how to breathe, and focusing on your breath is a simple way to bring kindness to yourself.

CHILD'S POSE

Balloon Breathing

So now, let's get ready to do this breathing practice. Go ahead and lie down on your back with your arms at your side or on your belly. If it's comfortable, please close your eyes or look down toward your toes.

1. Let the breath come and go in an easy, comfortable way.

2. Now place one hand under your nose. Notice the warm air on your hand as you breathe out.

3. Move your hand from your nose to your chest. Feel your chest rising and falling as you breathe in and breathe out.

4. Now move your hand to your belly and notice the breath filling the belly like a balloon filling up with air. If you like, you can fill your balloon with your favorite color as you breathe in.

5. As you breathe out, notice how your belly deflates like a balloon with no air.

6. See if you can pay attention to how the breath can soothe and relax you.

7. Now, keeping your attention on your belly rising and falling, breathe in and out three more times. Count each breath as you breathe out.

8. Now, let go of the meditation and just rest in your body, letting things be just as they are.

When you're ready, open your eyes and sit up.

You can download an audio track of this practice at http://www.newharbinger.com/50645.

Kindhearted Word Search

Find these kindhearted words in the word search underneath to remind yourself of what you learned in this chapter: compassion, breathe, friend, kindness, soothe, together, care, comfort, rainbow, hug, heart, belong.

COMPASSION

BREATHE

FRIEND

KINDNESS

SOOTHE

TOGETHER

CARE

COMFORT

RAINBOW

HUG

HEART

BELONG

```
            F Q K              G X J
          O C K W T          U I T L R
        M H E A R T D      H W S G E Q B
        T O G E T H E R B R E A T H E
        E R A I N B O W E H T O O S C
        N C O M F O R T F P H V C A X
        C O M P A S S I O N N K R A F
          L L H X P F T O I F E R R
          M Y V C G N O L E B Q I C
          W S S E N D N I K E X
          N O C W J W X N V
            B T U R Q D F
              M T A Y V
                D I R
                G
```

Here-and-Now Stone

In this chapter, you have learned what self-kindness and compassion are. Here is another easy activity you can do to help focus your attention and help calm your mind and body. But first you will need to find a small stone, one that will fit in the palm of your hand. Choose a stone that you like maybe because of its shape or color, or something about it.

How often do we pay attention to the stones we walk on every day? In this activity, you will be using your senses to explore every part of your stone. You may need to wash it off before you begin, so do that now if you want to.

Now, begin by bringing your attention to this stone, using your *sense of sight*. Notice the smoothness, the jagged edges, colors or patterns, and any other special qualities of your stone.

Now close your eyes and explore the stone with your *sense of touch*. First, close your hand around the stone and squeeze it. Is it hard or soft? Is it rough or smooth, does it have ridges, or is it round or flat? What is the temperature of the stone, warm or cool? You might want to keep your stone nearby to remind you to use your five senses.

Write down what you learned through your sense of sight and touch:

_____

_____

_____

MORE

Do you feel calm and quiet in your mind and body when you pay attention in this way? **Circle yes or no. YES   NO**

Some stones may be as old as the earth itself. You may want to take a moment to appreciate how long your stone has been around.

Now that you've been curious about your stone, put it away for now and draw as many details as you can remember about it in the space provided. When you're finished drawing, bring out your stone again and see how many details you remembered.

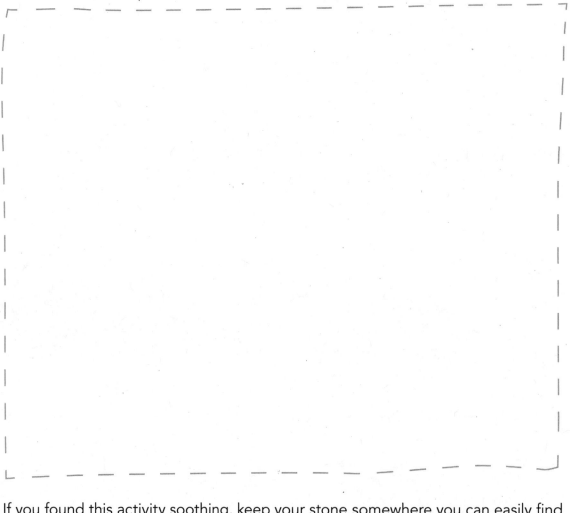

If you found this activity soothing, keep your stone somewhere you can easily find it, or carry it with you so you have it when you need it. You can do this activity anytime, anywhere, all on your own.

Building Your Toolkit

Now that you've learned what self-kindness and self-compassion are, you can choose how to be a friend to yourself, especially when you're faced with a challenge.

Check off the activities you learned in this chapter that you would like to try again.

___ Rainbow Breathing   ___ Soothing Touch   ___ Balloon Breathing

___ Follow the Rainbow   ___ Cat/Cow Yoga Pose   ___ Here-and-Now Stone

💗 SHARING IS CARING

What activities or ideas about self-compassion would you like to share with a friend? Write a friend's name and an activity or idea that you would like to share.

Your friend's name: _____

What would you like to share with them? _____

_____

_____

🔍 TO BE REVEALED

In the next chapter, you will discover for yourself how mindfulness can help you train your puppy mind to pay attention when you need to focus or concentrate.

CHAPTER 2

Paying Attention in a New Way

Have you ever noticed how your mind can jump around, making it hard to focus? Mindfulness is about paying attention moment by moment, becoming more alert to what is happening all around you, even inside your body. Mindfulness can teach you how to be curious and interested in what's here right now instead of being distracted by a daydream or a worry about the future. Through mindfulness practices, you can build your awareness muscle to help you stay connected to the present moment. For example, you can choose to pay attention to eating an apple through your five senses. When you use your sense of taste, touch, or even sound while eating, you may notice more about what it's like to eat an apple and you might even enjoy it more.

The more you practice mindfulness, the easier it is to focus your attention. Once you can focus your attention, you can also learn how to calm your mind and body. In this chapter, you will have a chance to build this awareness muscle through fun and exciting activities.

One way to begin building your awareness muscle is through your sense of hearing. In other words, you can learn how to pay attention to sound through your hearing. This is a great way to train your mind to focus on what is happening right now.

Sound Scavenger Hunt

Find a room to go to or a place to sit outside, with your parent or caregiver's permission. Find a good spot where you can sit and quietly wait for sounds to come to you. A good sound hunter can detect all kinds of sounds, so listen with your full attention.

Then share what sounds you found in this notebook.

Sound Scavenger Hunt Notebook

The farthest sound you could hear: _____

A loud sound: _____

A quiet sound: _____

The sound that lasted the longest: _____

A sound you enjoyed hearing: _____

A sound inside you: _____

ACTIVITY 12

Eating with All of Your Senses

In this activity, you get to use your imagination to pretend you are from another planet and you have never eaten any Earth food before. Even aliens have to eat, so select a food item like a piece of chocolate or some fruit and explore it with all of your senses to learn about this Earth food. Remember, you are new to the planet and you have never seen this food before. Paying attention with your senses is also another great way to build your mindfulness muscle!

Materials you will need: one piece of fruit or chocolate

Instructions:

1. Hold the earth food in your hand and close your eyes.

2. Use your fingers to *feel*. Notice the shape of your earth food. Notice the texture to see if it is bumpy or smooth.

3. Use your eyes to *see*. Notice the colors of your earth food. Notice the size and shape.

4. Use your nose to *smell*. Notice if it smells sweet. Notice if it has a strong smell or no smell at all.

5. Use your ears to *hear*. Hold it close to your ear. Squeeze or peel your earth food. Notice the sound it makes.

6. Use your tongue to *taste*. Place the food on your tongue. Take one bite and notice the taste. Begin chewing and notice how the taste changes. Notice what it feels like to swallow.

Silent Zombie Walk

We don't usually think of zombies as mindful. Quite the opposite! But pretending to walk like a zombie can be a fun way to practice mindful walking. When you pay attention to your body walking and the feeling of your feet on the ground, it can be a good way to calm the mind and body.

Start by standing up tall, and bring your attention all the way down into the soles of your feet. Now rock forward and back a little, and then side to side, noticing how your body doesn't let you fall and how helpful your feet are as they keep you standing.

Now, see if you can make your legs very stiff, and then begin to walk slowly, very slowly, walking like a zombie. Notice how different it is when you slow down. Notice all the changes in the soles of your feet as you take each step with stiff zombie legs.

See if you can walk like a zombie for ten steps forward and then ten steps back.

Now, you can make your arms stiff like a zombie. Lift them straight out in front of you. You might even make a sound like a zombie for the last few steps.

At the end of your walk, let your body relax and notice how your mind and body feel. **How was walking like a zombie different from the way you normally walk?**

_____

_____

_____

_____

How would it be helpful to slow down and pay attention to your body when you are walking?

_____

_____

_____

_____

You may have noticed that your mind was thinking about zombies or something else as you were doing the Silent Zombie Walk. The mind naturally wanders around when it isn't focusing on something specific. In the next activity, you can learn to train your mind.

Who Let the Puppy Out?

Have you ever seen how a new puppy behaves before it is trained? It wants to play, eat, and sleep whenever it wants. It has no idea about rules or where to use the bathroom. It thinks it can chew on anything. And, because it is so curious about the sights and smells in its environment, it can wander off and get lost. It simply doesn't know any better. It needs to be trained to become a good pet.

So, just like a puppy, your *busy mind* can wander off. It can begin to think about what happened yesterday or this morning or it can worry about what might happen tomorrow. And when this happens, it can keep you from paying attention when you need to, or it can even cause you some stress.

Can you think of a time when it would be good to focus and pay attention? Write it down here.

Now try this experiment to see how busy your puppy mind is.

1. Get comfortable wherever you are, and if it's okay, close your eyes.

2. Place one hand on your belly and one hand on your chest.

3. Now, anchor your attention on your breathing. This means keeping your attention on the breath. Feel your breath coming and going for a few breaths.

4. Now, feel your breath come into your chest and your belly and notice if they change.

5. Where is your puppy mind right now? Is it focusing on the breath or did it wander off? Can you bring your attention back to the breath?

6. Gently open your eyes.

Was your puppy mind able to pay attention to the breath? **Circle your answer:**

YES   NO

Was your puppy mind busy and paying attention to other things? **Circle your answer:**

YES   NO

If you like, you can draw a picture of what your puppy mind was doing.

Puppy Mind Jar

When you learn to focus your attention, you are being kind to yourself. Puppy minds are busy minds and can create stress and worry sometimes. Quiet minds allow you to rest and take care of yourself. Here is an experiment to show you the difference between a quiet mind and a busy puppy mind.

Materials you will need: baking soda, water, big jar with a lid

This experiment will show you how mindfulness can help settle and quiet your mind and help you stay focused on what's happening right now.

1. Fill the jar with water, leaving an inch at the top.

2. Add in half a cup of baking soda or sugar and close the lid tightly.

3. Shake the container and watch the jar become cloudy. This is what can happen in your mind when it gets busy, and there are lots of thoughts whizzing around, or when you get upset or stressed.

4. Remember, your puppy mind is always wandering to the past or the future unless you focus your attention.

5. Keep watching the cloudy water in the jar as the baking powder settles to the bottom. Notice how the water becomes clear again. Mindfulness can help settle your busy mind in the same way. As you focus your attention, the busy thoughts begin to settle just like the cloudy water, and you can clear your mind.

6. Shake the jar again and watch the jar as the cloudiness settles. This time, focus on your breathing as you watch the baking soda settle, and see what happens in your mind and body.

Use the image to the right to draw how busy or quiet your mind is now at the end of this activity. You can draw squiggly lines or choose another way to show how your mind is now.

Training Your Puppy Mind

You may have already noticed that focusing your attention can be challenging. Sometimes your puppy mind is very busy and needs help settling down and staying in place. There are times when your puppy mind needs help to focus, so here is a new and interesting way to train your attention.

1. Stretch your nonwriting hand outward like a five-pointed star with your palm facing toward you.

2. Now take the pointer finger of your writing hand and begin to trace from the base of the thumb to the top of the thumb, inhaling and counting to one, and then exhaling slowly down the other side of the thumb.

3. Slide your tracing finger up the pointer finger of your star hand, inhaling, and when you reach the top, saying two, and then exhaling as you slide your finger slowly down the other side.

4. Repeat this same inhaling, tracing, counting, and exhaling for each finger until you reach the end or base of the little finger.

5. And, then going in reverse, continue tracing, inhaling, counting, and exhaling, up the little finger and down the other side, then the next finger, and so on, until you return to the end of the thumb again.

How busy was your puppy mind during this activity? **Circle the number that shows how quiet your puppy was at the end of the exercise.**

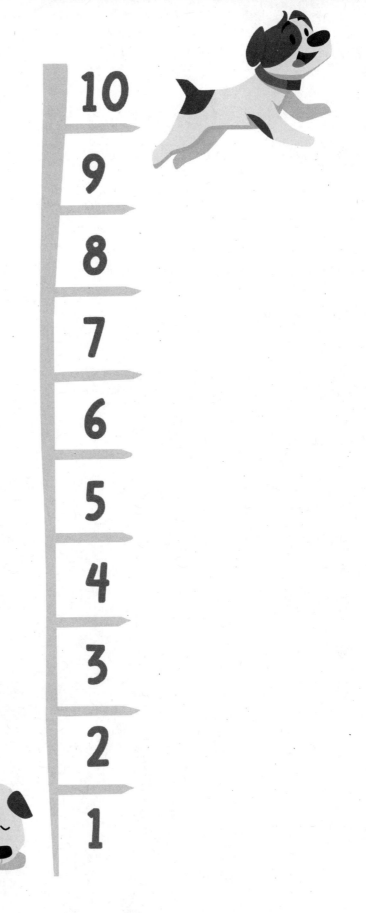

ACTIVITY 17

Searching with a Focused Puppy Mind

mindful

Look at the image of a farm.

Use your sense of sight to pay careful attention, so you can find all the words you have learned about mindfulness hidden in the farm. Here is another way to build your mindfulness muscle.

The hidden words are:

- puppy mind
- zombie
- breathe
- attention
- mindful

zombie

puppy mind

33

A Reminder to Breathe

Read the acrostic poem on the next page that spells out the word BREATHE, and draw a picture of yourself below that goes with this poem. Or if you prefer, you can make your own acrostic poem of BREATHE using your own words.

Busy mind

Restless body

Enjoy a breath

Anchor attention

To this moment

Here and now

Easy, flowing breath

Compassionate Body Scan

In this chapter, you've practiced paying attention in a new way and learned how to settle and quiet your busy puppy mind. Now you can use these skills to become more aware of your body and learn to bring kindness to yourself.

1. Begin by getting comfortable lying on your back or sitting right where you are.

2. Now pay attention to your breathing, noticing how your body breathes naturally…the belly rising and falling with each breath, just as it did in the Balloon Breathing meditation in chapter 1.

3. When you're ready, move your attention down into your feet and legs and begin to notice any physical sensations, such as coolness or warmth.

4. Now, see if you can bring a little kindness to these legs, ankles, and knees for all the hard work they do every day, carrying you from one place to another.

5. Now move your attention from your legs up into your body, noticing your belly rising and falling and your lungs expanding and contracting, and appreciating these parts of your body.

6. Notice your heart beating and all the hard work it is doing. Thank your heart for the hard work it is doing.

7. If you notice that your puppy mind is wandering and thinking of something, gently return your attention to your body.

8. Now, move your attention to your arms, hands, and fingers, noticing how they feel, and be aware of how they allow you to touch, hold, create, and connect with others.

9. If you notice any pain in your body, like soreness or a bruise or maybe a headache, bring some compassion and warmth to this part of your body. You might place your hand on the part that is having a hard time and offer it a soothing gesture.

10. And finally pay attention to your head. Feel the heaviness of your skull and how well it protects your brain. Then see if you can notice the muscles around your eyes, your mouth, and jaw. Can you relax these parts of your face?

11. Can you take a final moment to have compassion and gratitude for this amazing body you live in? You might want to thank your body for all the hard work it does to keep you safe and strong.

Gently open your eyes and draw a heart or a Band-Aid in the picture on the next page in the place where your body needs kind attention. Use a smiley face symbol for where your body feels relaxed. Draw a thumbs-up for a part of your body you appreciate.

MORE →

Building Your Toolkit

Now that you've learned what mindfulness is, you can use it to help calm your mind and body.

Put a check mark next to the activities you learned in this chapter that you would like to try again:

___ Sound Scavenger Hunt

___ Eating with All of Your Senses

___ Silent Zombie Walk

___ Who Let the Puppy Out?

___ Puppy Mind Jar

___ Training Your Puppy Mind

___ Searching with a Focused Puppy Mind

___ A Reminder to Breathe

___ Compassionate Body Scan

♥ SHARING IS CARING

What activities or ideas about mindfulness would you like to share with a friend? Write a friend's name and an activity or idea that you would like to share.

Your friend's name: _____

What would you like to share with them? _____

_____

_____

🔍 TO BE REVEALED

In the next chapter, you will discover more ways to be kind to yourself—skills that will help you become a good friend to yourself.

CHAPTER 3

Growing Kindness

Have you ever wondered why your parents, teachers, and maybe even coaches talk about how important kindness is? It's because they know that kindness helps build good friendships and good feelings. Kindness is a way of being friendly, generous, and caring to yourself and to those near and far. Think about the last time you were kind to someone. Do you remember how it made you feel? If you felt good, it's because your brain releases "happy chemicals" that create positive feelings when you are kind and caring to others and yourself.

In this chapter, you will learn how important it is to be kind to yourself as well as others. Treating yourself the way you would treat a good friend helps you build your kindness muscle and makes you stronger. Think about how it feels when you're hurt or sad. You might notice that you feel like giving up, but as you practice self-kindness, you can feel the power of kindness strengthening your brave heart! Kindness is a *superpower* that helps you care, connect, and crush challenges!

Planting Seeds of Kindness

Planting seeds in a pot is a great way to grow kindness. Your plant will need you to care for it by making sure it has the proper nutrients to help it grow, like water and sunlight. Plants, just like you, need kind words.

Did you know that loving-kindness can help you grow new brain cells to power your positive emotions and to connect to others? And when you show kindness to any living being, it can help them grow healthy and strong too.

Materials you will need: small three- or five-inch pot, packet of seeds (flower or vegetable), small bag of potting soil or some dirt from your garden, stickers, markers, paints (optional)

Instructions:

To begin, you can decorate your pot using markers or paints to write some of the surrounding words on it. Choose  words that show what you would like to grow in your own heart. You can use images or symbols as well and add stickers to help decorate your pot.

Once you have decorated your pot, put the soil in and plant your seeds. Add just a little water to quench their thirst. Remember to water and give them the right amount of sunlight to help your seeds grow, just as you are growing kindness in your heart.

Here is another way to plant seeds of kindness. You can decorate this image with these same words if you don't have a pot and seeds available.

43

A-Mazing Facts
About Kindness

Now, it's time to take your puppy mind on a walk through the maze to see how well trained it is. Can you focus your attention all the way through the maze and collect the facts about kindness as you go? Then answer the question at the end of the journey.

START
HERE

Question at the end of the journey: What was your favorite fact about kindness? Circle the fact in the maze or write down your favorite fact here.

_____

_____

_____

Kindness . . .

HELPS US FEEL LIKE WE BELONG

HELPS US CARE FOR OTHERS

MAKES US FEEL GOOD

Makes parts of the brain stronger and helps us worry less

Makes us happier

MAKES THE WORLD A BETTER PLACE

END HERE

Breathing Kindness with a Pinwheel

Here is a chance to notice the power of your breath by breathing on a pinwheel. First you need to make your own pinwheel.

Materials you will need: paper or card stock, scissors, glue stick, crayons or markers, pushpin, bead with a hole or small button, pencil eraser

Instructions:

1. Cut out two 7-inch squares from thick paper or card stock. You can also download the template at http://www.newharbinger.com/50645 and print out. The squares can be any color you choose.

2. Draw some patterns or designs on the squares if you like. Bring all your attention to your decorating.

3. Cut out both paper squares with attention and mindfulness. You can ask a parent or caregiver or another adult for help if you need it.

4. Glue the undecorated sides of the squares carefully together so that the edges line up and you end up with one flat square with decorations on both sides. Let the glue dry before going to step 5.

5. Cut four diagonal lines starting from the corners and cutting halfway to the center of the square. Ask for help if you need it.

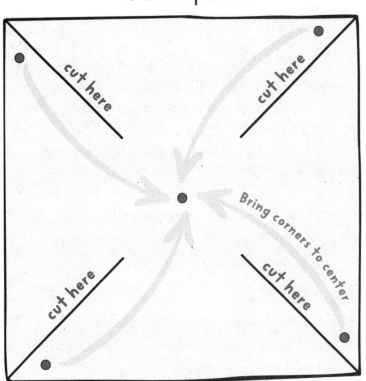

7-inch square

cut here

cut here

cut here

cut here

Bring corners to center

6. Take one of the corner tips and bend it toward the center of the square without creasing the paper. You can glue the tip in place or just hold it there with your hand.

7. Now bend the opposite tip toward the center of the square, and then do the same with the other two corners. You should now have all four tips at the center of the square.

8. Insert a pushpin through the four tips at the center of the wheel to hold them together.

9. Turn over the wheel and put the pin point through a button or a bead, if you are using one. Then push the point of the pin it into the pencil eraser. Make sure the eraser is far enough from the wheel so it can spin easily.

Now blow on the pinwheel. Notice how your breath makes the wheel spin. You can use your pinwheel to help you practice your mindful breathing. You can also imagine that your pinwheel is spreading kindness throughout the world. You can think of a friend who might need extra kindness right now, or just send kindness to someone in your school or someone else you care about, just because you can!

Loving-Kindness for Someone You Care About

In this short meditation, you can use kind wishes to calm and soothe yourself while building your kindness muscle toward others. Sometimes it's hard to think about someone you want to send good wishes to. If you find that it is difficult for you to come up with someone, it's okay. You can always just breathe in a kind word for yourself if things don't feel so easy.

1. Take a moment to get comfortable, either lying down or sitting in a comfortable chair. Then, close your eyes and think about someone you care about, someone who makes you smile and makes you feel good inside when you think about them!

2. Now, picture this person clearly in your mind. It can be a friend, grandparent, parent, or your brother or sister, or even your pet. Take a moment to pause with this picture of them in mind.

3. Now bring your hand to your heart or give yourself a hug and imagine that you are offering this special person or pet a warm hug.

4. Think about how happy it makes them feel when you hold them close to your heart. Imagine the smile on their face.

5. Just take your time…notice what you are feeling inside as you imagine giving this special friend or pet your kind attention.

6. Picture yourself with this friend as you send them these kind wishes: "I wish you happiness. I wish you kindness. I wish you friendship." Repeat these wishes a couple of times.

7. And now just pay attention to how it feels to send good wishes to someone you care about, maybe just naming the feeling to yourself in silence.

8. When you're ready, open your eyes.

To whom did you send kind wishes? _____

Notice if this meditation helped you feel more caring or connected to this person. **Circle the emoji below that best shows how you feel now.**

What Does Kindness Look Like?

Now that you have practiced sending kind wishes to someone you care about, let's explore other ways to show kindness. **Look at the Kindness Chart and choose one act of kindness you would like to do this week.** You can also write in acts of kindness that you would like to do in the blank spaces. Feel free to color in this chart and hang it on your wall or on your refrigerator to help remind you of the many ways you can bring kindness to this world! Don't forget about yourself!

You can download this template at http://www.newharbinger.com/50645 and print it out.

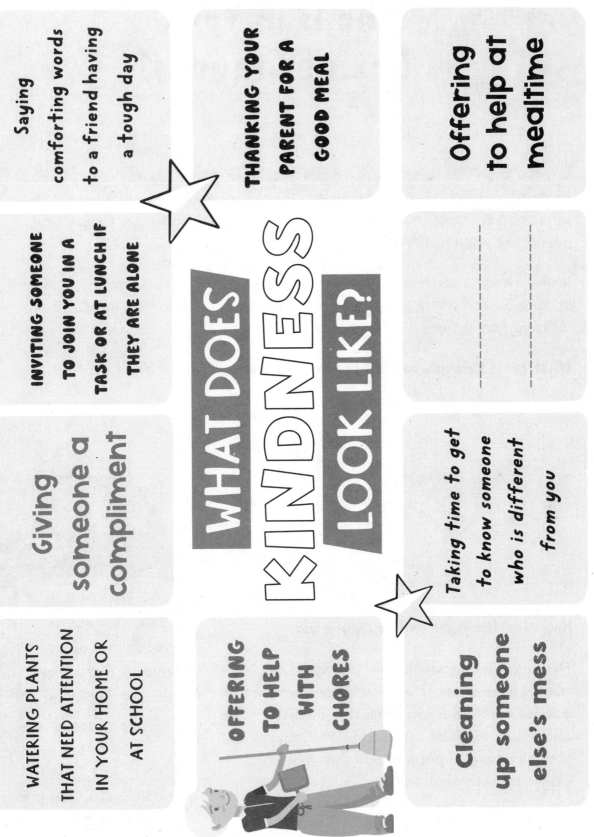

WHAT DOES KINDNESS LOOK LIKE?

Saying comforting words to a friend having a tough day

THANKING YOUR PARENT FOR A GOOD MEAL

Offering to help at mealtime

INVITING SOMEONE TO JOIN YOU IN A TASK OR AT LUNCH IF THEY ARE ALONE

Giving someone a compliment

Taking time to get to know someone who is different from you

WATERING PLANTS THAT NEED ATTENTION IN YOUR HOME OR AT SCHOOL

OFFERING TO HELP WITH CHORES

Cleaning up someone else's mess

Who Is in Your Box of Crayons?

Did you know that science says it is easier to be kind to people who seem to be more like you? For example, if they look like you, dress like you, or even eat the same food as you, it's easier to be nice to them. But being kind to people who are not like you is just as important. Maybe more so!

Imagine a world where everyone was just like everyone else. Boring, right? Now imagine a world where everyone was kind to everyone else, even those who are different from them!

What could help you be kind to those who are different from you?

_____

_____

_____

_____

Now read the poem on the crayon box.

This poem helps you see what you would be missing if there was only one color of crayon in the box. Having more colors can make your world more colorful! It's the same with people. Including people who are different from you can make your world bigger, more colorful, and more fun.

"We are a box of crayons, each one of us unique. But, when we get together, the picture is complete."

—DeRolf

Can you think of four kids in your world who are different from you? For example, you might have a friend who likes sports when you like video games or someone who speaks a different language than you. **Draw on the crayons below what you appreciate about these kids, and color the crayons however you wish!**

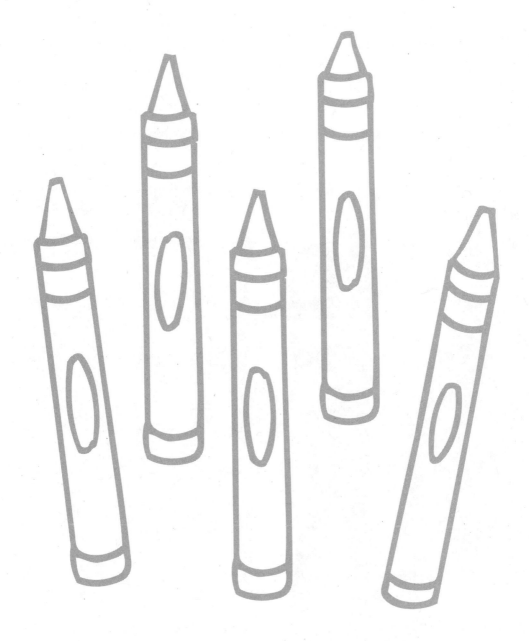

What About You?

Now that you know more about the importance of including others in your circle of kindness, here are some fun ways to practice being kind to yourself!

Start by remembering what it's like when you treat yourself with kindness.

What are three ways you are already kind to yourself?

1. _____

2. _____

3. _____

A Clue for You to Undo

Solve the riddle and make yourself rich! Use the number grid decoder to help you answer the question.

Riddle: *What is free, yet priceless?*

K __ __ __ __ __ __ __
3-1   2-4   3-4   1-4   3-4   1-5   4-4   4-4

Here are helpful instructions for using the decoder:

Step 1: Find the two numbers under the first blank line (3-1) above.

Step 2: Find the first number (3) on the left side of the grid below.

Step 3: Find the second number (1) along the top of the grid.

Step 4: See if you can find the letter in the grid where these two numbers meet (K).

Step 5: The first blank line has been filled in for you. Now it is your turn to complete the rest of the blanks until you have found the answer.

	1	2	3	4	5
1	A	B	C	D	E
2	F	G	H	I	J
3	K	L	M	N	O
4	P	Q	R	S	T
5	U	V	W	X	Y

A Kind Wishes Tree

Kind words can help you be a good friend to yourself. Knowing what kind words you would like to hear can help you uncover your brave heart and find strength when you need it.

Here is a simple way to turn kind words into a good wish for yourself. Choose as many wishes as you like from the "Kind Wishes Tree for Me" list below, or create your own good wishes. You can begin by asking yourself *What words would I most like to hear every day?*

Kind Wishes Tree Just for Me

"I wish to feel calm."

"I wish to be happy."

"I wish to be brave."

"I wish to feel strong."

"I wish to belong."

"I wish to be a good friend."

"I wish to feel safe."

"I wish to be feel accepted."

"I wish to be loved."

Hang your wishes on the tree. These are wishes you can send to yourself...and remember, you are listening to whatever you say to yourself, so choose wisely.

"Kind Wishes Just for Me" Meditation

You can practice saying kind wishes aloud to yourself. This is a way of creating a positive new habit! Notice how the words calm and soothe you when you are upset. You can also download an audio track of this meditation at http://www. newharbinger.com/50645. Listen to the recording and practice saying your kind wishes.

1. Close your eyes and get comfortable. If it feels right for you, place your hand on your heart or any place that helps you feel calm and cared about.

2. Now follow your breath in through your nose, moving down into your chest, and into your belly and out again.

3. If your hand is on your heart, see if you can begin to notice how hand, heart, and breath move together. Take a pause.

4. Now, ask yourself, *What words would be helpful for me to hear when I'm upset or having a hard time?* Maybe you have already come up with kind words that you need to hear. Or maybe there are words that you've heard from your parents or grandparents that you would like to remember. These words are for you only, no one else. Make them your own. Plant them in your heart. For example: *May I know I am strong. May I feel brave. May I feel peaceful and calm.*

5. Say your words to yourself two more times slowly to make sure they are planted in your heart.

6. Now, resting in your body, notice your breathing.

7. Just let yourself enjoy the good feeling of sending good wishes to yourself.

If you like, you can think of a few times when you would most like to hear these kind words for yourself, and write these times down here.

1. ____

2. ____

3. ____

You can download an audio track of this practice at http://www.newharbinger.com/50645.

Walking with Wishes in the Woods

Sending good wishes to a plant or an animal in nature is another way to help you build your brave and kind heart. You can take a walk around your neighborhood or in a forest, on the beach, or even on a trail in the mountains with permission from your parent or caregiver. As you walk, notice the sights and sounds around you.

When you hear or see an animal, a plant, or a tree that is interesting, take a moment to give them your full attention. You might imagine you have the sharp eyes of a hawk or the supersensitive ears of a deer.

Send a kind wish to whatever you discover. All plants and creatures need kindness. For example, you might say, "May you live a long and a healthy life."

You might also feel gratitude for all the ways that nature helps you, like providing shade with its canopy of leaves or cleaning the air you breathe.

If you like, you can bring home something that you find along your walk, like a feather or a leaf, and paste it into this workbook, or you can draw something you discovered.

In the space provided, take some time to draw or paste what you discovered on your walk and write about your discovery and about the kind wishes you sent out into nature.

Cobra Yoga Pose

One way to practice self-care is through movement. Here is a yoga pose that can help you strengthen your back and open your brave heart. It can help in moments of stress and is a great way to be kind to your mind, body, and heart.

1. Start by lying on your belly with your legs straight behind you and the tops of your feet resting flat on the floor (or you can use a yoga mat).

2. Place your hands flat on the floor next to your shoulders and spread your fingers wide.

3. Press your hands down into the floor and straighten your arms as you use your back muscles to lift up your chest.

4. As you press your legs and feet into the floor, lengthen your whole front body upward, like a cobra, while looking up toward the sky.

5. Breathe two to four breaths and gently lie back down to rest, resting your head on one cheek.

6. Repeat the pose one more time and then rest your head on the opposite cheek.

Take a moment to appreciate how you can move like a cobra to make your body long and strong!

Building Your Toolkit

You now have more tools for being kind to yourself and to other kids and to all living things in nature.

Put a check mark next to the activities you learned in this chapter that you would like to try again:

___ Planting Seeds of Kindness

___ A-Mazing Facts About Kindness

___ Breathing Kindness with a Pinwheel

___ Loving-Kindness for Someone You Care About

___ What Does Kindness Look Like?

___ Who Is in Your Box of Crayons?

___ What About You?

___ A Clue for You to Undo

___ A Kind Wishes Tree

___ "Kind Wishes Just for Me" Meditation

___ Walking with Wishes in the Woods

___ Cobra Yoga Pose

 SHARING IS CARING

What activities or ideas about kindness would you like to share with a friend? Write a friend's name and an activity or idea that you would like to share.

Your friend's name: _____

What would you like to share with them? _____

_____

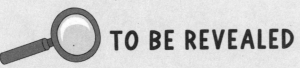 TO BE REVEALED

In the next chapter, you will discover for yourself how compassion can comfort you and connect you to others in helpful, healthy ways. It is a superpower that will last forever!

CHAPTER 4

Compassion Is Your Superpower

Have you ever been with a friend who got hurt in some way; maybe they got their feelings hurt or got sick? It's not always easy to know how to help others when they're having a hard time. But, there is a superpower that you can strengthen to help you in times like these. This superpower is called *compassion*, and it's one way you can show others that you care about them. Compassion is a way of being a friend to others. Using this superpower of caring for yourself and others makes the world a better place and builds a better brain!

An important part of compassion is to recognize when someone else is struggling. We can tell others might be struggling because we can feel what they feel. Did you know feelings can be "contagious"? Your brain knows just how to help you catch what others are feeling. This is called *empathy*, and in this chapter, you get to see your own empathy in action. The supersensitive brain cells that trigger empathy can also help you see things from another person's point of view. The more empathy you have, the more you boost your brain's ability to build the superpower of compassion!

Just so you know, there are two sides to compassion. The tender side of compassion is something you already know. It's the loving, kind, and gentle side of compassion you learned about in chapter 1. The other side of compassion is what allows you to be fierce and strong when you need to be (Neff 2021). In this chapter, you will get to discover the fierce side of compassion that can motivate and protect you in times of need.

How Do You Know What Others Are Feeling?

Empathy is a special power in your brain that allows you to feel what others are feeling. For example, when your friend is hurt or disappointed, you can actually feel their disappointment, even though you might not always be aware of feeling their feelings. Empathy is like stepping into someone else's shoes and seeing things from their point of view.

How does this happen? We have special cells in our brains that reflect back to you what another person is feeling, just like a mirror reflects your own image back to you. These mirror neurons allow you to feel the same feeling as someone else. These same mirror neurons can also encourage you to imitate someone else's behavior, like yawning. You may have noticed that when you see someone yawn, it makes you yawn too.

Solve the word puzzle below:

Hold this workbook page up to a mirror.

Read the word below in the mirror.

Write it in the line underneath.

EWbΑΤΗΥ

The Amazing Powers of Empathy

Read the acrostic poem to see how empathy helps you make the world a better place!

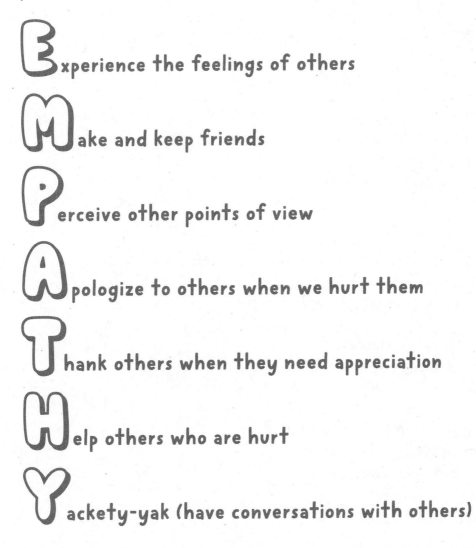

Experience the feelings of others

Make and keep friends

Perceive other points of view

Apologize to others when we hurt them

Thank others when they need appreciation

Help others who are hurt

Yackety-yak (have conversations with others)

Color in the letters that spell empathy and circle the abilities in the acrostic that will help to strengthen you.

ACTIVITY 34

Cloud Gazing

Have you ever done cloud gazing? Watching clouds is such an amazing way to use your imagination! This is especially fun on a windy day when clouds are moving quickly and forming different shapes. Cloud gazing with a friend happens to be a great way to practice seeing things from another person's point of view.

Do this activity with a friend:

Lie down on a bed of grass, or if it's too cold, you can lie down on the floor inside your house, but make sure you have a good view of the sky and the clouds passing by.

As you watch the clouds moving, take turns with your friend pointing out cloud formations and sharing what they look like to you.

When one of you shares what they see, the other one can try to see the same thing. Your friend may need to point out where they see the image in the clouds.

Keep watching to see how the shape changes and what new form it can take.

After you finish cloud gazing, use this space to draw the figures both you and your friend were able to discover in the clouds.

Draw here

Finding Your Way into the Hearts of Others

After learning about empathy, you're now ready to boost your superpower of compassion.

Empathy is a way of seeing things from another person's perspective.

Compassion is the way you can show others that you care about them. Using this superpower to care for others makes the world a better place! **In the heart shape, write in the name of someone you think could use some care right now.** While you hold this person in your heart, send them a kind wish as you color in the heart image.

Growing Your Circle of Compassion

A circle of compassion is one way you can bring all those you care about into your heart. This circle of compassion activity gives you a chance to name all the people who are important to you. This can include people in your family, your friends, and even others who are far away.

Compassion can help everyone all around the world. All kids are alike and have similar wishes for themselves, even if they look different or speak a different language. Knowing how all kids are similar and have similar wishes for themselves makes it easier to include them in your circle of compassion.

So, now you get to create your own circle of compassion.

In the three circles:

1. Draw all those you feel closest to in the center.

2. In the next circle outward, draw others you care about but maybe don't know as well. You can include parts of nature or animals too!

3. In the outer circle, draw other people from other cultures or countries around the world that you know about.

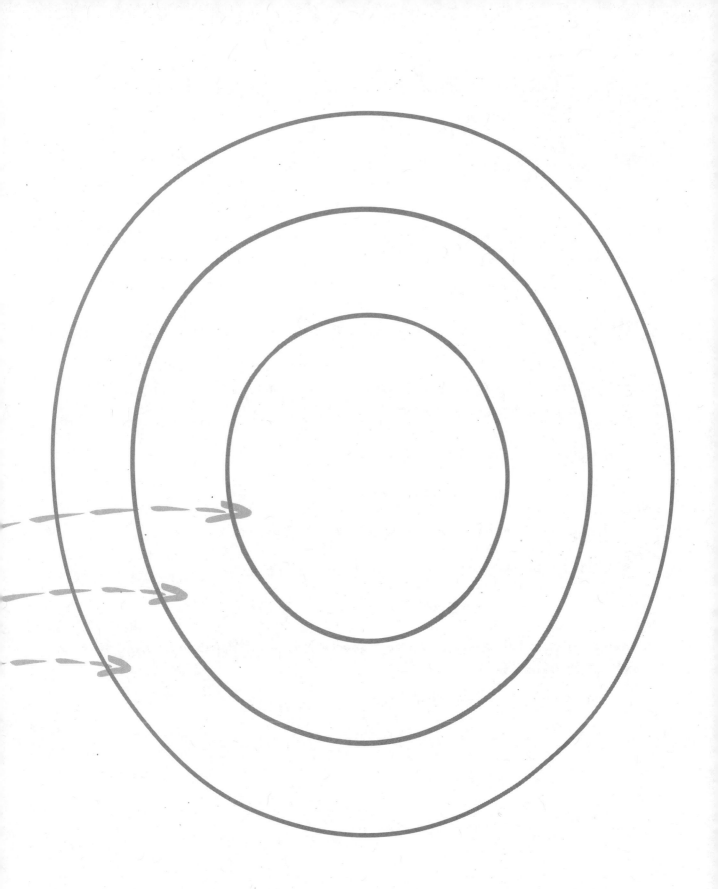

"A Kid Just Like Me" Meditation

Here is a chance for you to see how all kids have things in common and have similar wishes for themselves, even if they look different and live far away. Knowing this can make it easier to include them in your circle of compassion.

Instructions:

Lie down and get comfortable, and close your eyes if you wish. Take a few deep breaths to calm yourself, and bring to mind a friend or someone you know. Then consider a few things about this kid:

This kid is a human being…just like me.

This kid has feelings and thoughts…just like me.

This kid has been hurt, angry, sad, or disappointed…just like me.

This kid wants to have friends and be happy…just like me.

This kid wants to be safe, healthy, and loved…just like me.

Open your eyes and write down how you felt or what happened during this part of the exercise.

_____

_____

_____

Now, close your eyes again and see if you can send this kid some good wishes:

I wish that this kid could be brave and strong.

I wish for this kid to know they are cared about by friends and family.

I wish for this kid to believe in him or herself.

I wish for this kid to be happy because this kid deserves to be happy…just like me.

Gently open your eyes when you feel ready. **Take a moment now to write in the heart image the wish that you most want to send to this person.**

Do you think it could be helpful if we all sent good wishes to others every day?

Boat Pose with a Partner

As you know, boats need to balance in the water, so they don't flip over. In this activity, you get to practice balancing like a boat. It's a fun way to strengthen your muscles and strengthen your connection to others. As you balance, see if you can tell which muscles you need to balance. Hint: they're the muscles that help you sit up straight at your desk.

Ask someone to be your partner for this exercise.

1. Sit across from your partner with your feet on the floor and your knees bent.

2. Place your hands on the floor behind your hips while you bring the soles of your feet together with your partner's.

3. Now, both of you, lift your feet off the ground with soles pressing into your partner's feet.

4. First use your hands to keep from falling over. Then, keeping your knees bent, reach for your partner's hands, one at a time.

5. As you hold on to each other's hands, both of you lean back and lift your chests up, and see if you can straighten your legs upward, keeping your feet pressed together.

6. As you imagine your boat gliding down the stream, see if you can straighten your legs, keeping the soles of the feet pressing into one another.

7. Notice what muscles you are using now.

8. Now, bend your knees again and put your feet on the floor and let go of your partner's hands.

9. Try this Boat pose one or two more times and see if it gets easier each time!

10. Lie on your back and rest. You deserve it!

If you want to try balancing your boat on your own, try this:

1. Sit on the ground with your legs straight and hands behind your hips on the floor to begin.

2. Bend your knees and lift your feet off the ground, placing your arms straight out in front of you with the palms facing each other.

3. When you can begin to, straighten your legs. (You can also use the help of a wall by placing your feet on the wall with legs held out straight in front of you.)

4. Then, slowly, one at a time, move your arms next to your legs and lift your chest.

Sometimes you have to ease yourself into a challenging pose like this if you are doing it alone. Don't give up…balancing is important to many things in life!

Circle the body parts you noticed that made the boat pose easier:

- Tummy
- Back
- Arms
- Face
- Toes
- Fingers
- Head
- Chest
- Lungs
- Legs
- Feet
- Nose

Compassion Creates Connection

Just being there for someone when they are having a difficult time can help to strengthen your connection to them, and it can make you feel better too!

You can create a compassion bracelet you can wear yourself or give as a gift to someone else you care about or who cares about you.

Materials you will need:
3 separate foot-long, half-inch-wide strips of cloth from an old T-shirt, scissors sharp enough for cutting cloth, clipboard or something to hold cloth strips in place.

1/2 inch strips

You may want to ask a parent or caregiver or another adult for help with cutting the cloth strips.

Instructions:

1. Take your strips of cloth and make a knot of the three strips at the end of the strips.

2. Clip the knot to the top of a clipboard.

3. Braid the three pieces together: Spread the three strips apart before beginning to braid. Take the left strip and cross it over the center strip. Take the right strip and cross it over the one that's in the center. Go back and forth from left to right, crossing over the middle strip each time.

When you get to the end, unclip the knot and tie both sides of the bracelet together in a knot at the right length for you to wear.

4. Then tie a second knot and cut off the excess fabric.

TO BRAID:
Bring left over center, then right over center. Repeat!

Did you notice how weaving the strips together made the material for the bracelet stronger than just a single strip alone was? This bracelet is a reminder of how compassion connects you to others and strengthens you.

Heart-to-Heart Breathing

Heart breathing with a friend or someone you care about is another way to tune into how someone else might be doing. As you sit with your partner, notice how it feels to breathe together. And if you would like to send this person good wishes, you can simply send a kind thought as you breathe out. Be sure to include yourself if you notice you might need a kind wish. You can breathe in kindness for yourself and breathe out kindness for your partner.

1. Sit on the ground cross-legged or with knees bent as you rest your back against your partner's back.

2. Put one hand on your belly and one hand on your chest. Take a deep breath; breathe in and out.

3. Notice how your chest and belly rise and fall with each breath.

4. See if you can do this two more times. Pause.

5. Now, as you continue to breathe, see if you can feel your partner's breath. Can you feel their breathing? Can you hear their breathing? Can you feel their back expand and contract as you breathe?

6. Now, see if you can breathe together. Try matching your breathing with your partner's. Pause.

7. As you continue breathing, see if you can breathe in a little kindness or compassion for yourself, and as you breathe out, see if you can send some kindness or compassion to your partner. Pause.

8. Notice how it feels to breathe together and for each other.

9. Open your eyes, and give your partner a high five!

What was it like to breathe with someone else, back-to-back?

_____

_____

_____

Now, circle the emotions that describe how you felt at the end of this breathing practice:

HAPPY   RESTED   Connected

WARM   EXCITED

Or write in your own words how you felt:

— — — — — — — — — — — — —   — — — — — — — — — —

Tender Vs. Fierce Compassion

In the practice you just did, you had a chance to experience *tender compassion*, which allows you to be gentle and accepting of yourself and others. But this is only one side of compassion. The other side makes you strong and helps you to say no to things that are harmful for you. This kind of compassion allows you to take action to stand up for yourself and for others when you need to or to make changes that support your well-being. It's called *fierce compassion*. It's kind of like having your own fierce momma bear inside you (Neff 2021).

Take a look at the images of the two bears. One is tender and one is fierce. **Draw a line from each example of compassion below and match it to the correct bear.**

- Giving myself or a friend a hug

- Saying no to something that is bad for you or others

- Standing up for a friend who is being bullied

- Encouraging yourself or others with kind words

- Doing a soothing breath practice to calm yourself

- Standing up to protect the environment

A Clue to Your Brave Heart

Use the decoder below to help you discover a final message for you in this chapter. The answer is at the bottom of this page.

Decoder:

A	B	C	D	E	F	G	H	I	J	K	L	M
1	2	3	4	5	6	7	8	9	10	11	12	13

N	O	P	Q	R	S	T	U	V	W	X	Y	Z
14	15	16	17	18	19	20	21	22	23	24	25	26

Message for you:

___ ___ ___ ___ ___ ___ ___ ___ ___ ___   ___ ___   ___ ___
   3-15-13-16-1-19-19-9-15-14   9-19   13-25

___ ___ ___ ___ ___ ___ ___ ___ ___
19-21-16-5-18-16-15-23-5-18

Decoder message: Compassion is my superpower.

Building Your Toolkit

Now you've learned how to build your compassion muscle and use this superpower to care for others.

Put a check mark next to the activities you learned in this chapter that you would like to try again:

___ How Do You Know What Others Are Feeling?

___ The Amazing Powers of Empathy

___ Cloud Gazing

___ Finding Your Way into the Hearts of Others

___ Growing Your Circle of Compassion

___ "A Kid Just Like Me" Meditation

___ Boat Pose with a Partner

___ Compassion Creates Connection

___ Heart-to-Heart Breathing

___ Tender Vs. Fierce Compassion

___ A Clue to Your Brave Heart

 ## SHARING IS CARING

What activities or ideas about compassion would you like to share with a friend? Write a friend's name and an activity or idea that you would like to share.

Your friend's name: _____

What would you like to share with them? _____

_____

TO BE REVEALED

Now it's time to meet your superhero. In the next chapter, you can see two important parts of yourself: the inner bully and the superhero. Your superhero is your champion and has great skills for protecting you!

CHAPTER 5

Your Inner Bully Meets Your Superhero

Now that you have had a chance to explore ways to be kind to yourself, are you ready to discover how kindness and compassion can be a superpower to help you deal with your inner bully? In this chapter, you will get to know two parts of yourself: your strong, powerful superhero and the inner bully. The inner bully is the part that can embarrass you or even make you feel sad when things go wrong. Once you get to know this inner bully, then you will learn how to tame it with the help of your superhero. This is how you can become a good friend to yourself!

ACTIVITY 43

Getting to Know Your Inner Bully

Your inner bully means well, but it doesn't always know the best way to help. Here is an example of what an inner bully might sound like when you don't get things done:

Billy thinks: *Wow, I have so much homework, and I don't want to do it.*

Billy's inner bully tells him: *Don't be so lazy. You're going to fail if you don't do it.*

In this activity, you will have a chance to get to know more about what your own inner bully has to say!

Circle a time when your inner bully might show up:

- Getting a bad grade
- Getting into a fight with a friend
- Not finishing chores
- Making a mistake

Or come up with another example:

Can you think of what your inner bully said when something like this went wrong and you got really upset with yourself? Here are some examples of what your inner bully might say to you:

- *You really messed up.*

- *No one is going to like you.*

- *You should have tried harder.*

- *This is why you get into trouble!*

Write in the speech bubbles what the inner bully said to you the last time you were upset.

Getting the Inner Bully Out of Your Head

So now do a sketch of what your inner bully might look like. You can use pencils or pens or crayons, or whatever your favorite sketching tool is. You might draw your inner bully as a person, an animal, or a comic book character. Your sketch can show how strong, large, or powerful your inner bully seems to you. This can help you make room for the other parts of yourself that have a kinder and more supportive way of encouraging you.

Draw your inner bully here:

Three Soothing Breaths

Now that you know what your inner bully sounds and looks like, try this easy breathing practice to let the inner bully go. This is a simple practice of *breathing in* and *breathing out*. Focusing your attention on your breath like this can help you calm your inner bully and calm your body by quieting the part of the brain that causes you to feel stress.

1. Sit still and close your eyes or, if it feels better to you, you can keep your eyes open just a little and look down toward your knees.

2. Notice your breathing and how your belly rises and falls as the breath comes in and out.

3. You may notice that your puppy mind begins to wander during this exercise, so see if you can focus your attention on just one whole breath.

4. Now, see if you can focus your attention on three breaths in a row. Count each breath as you breathe in and let out it out with a big sigh.

5. When you have finished your three breaths, gently open your eyes.

Do you feel different after these three soothing breaths? Taking soothing breaths is a way to be kind to yourself when you need it, like when your inner bully is being unkind to you.

Remember, this is a practice you can do anytime, anywhere.

You can download an audio track of this practice at http://www.newharbinger.com/50645.

A New Way of Seeing

Learning to calm the inner bully helps you connect to your superhero. Your superhero is the part of you that wants you to do well, and it can help you see things in new ways.

Choose one of the following activities to help you see things differently, and spend a few minutes doing it:

- Use a magnifying glass to investigate something you see every day, like a blade of grass, a worm, a pencil, clean toilet paper, or dirt on your socks. What do you see? How does the object change when you look through the magnifying glass?

- Lie on the ground and look upward toward the sky. How does your view change when you are in this position?

- Lie on your bed with your head hanging off slightly. What do you see when you look at things upside down?

- Lie on the ground on your belly and imagine you're a worm. What do you see?

- Close your eyes. When you open them, see if you can notice four new things you've never seen before. Try this indoors and outdoors.

 What did you see differently? Describe one thing that surprised you or made you curious.

Viewfinder for Seeing Things in a New Way

Here's another way to practice seeing things in a new way.

Materials you will need: five-by-seven-inch mailing envelope, scissors, colored cellophane, markers, stickers, or anything else to help decorate the envelope

Instructions:

1. In the middle of the envelope, draw a circle that is at least as big as the circle you can make when you put your thumb and index finger together. You can make it a little bigger if you like.

2. Fold the envelope in the middle of the circle and make a small cut with your scissors inside the circle at the fold. You may want to ask a parent or caregiver or another adult for help with using the scissors. When you unfold the envelope, there will be a small hole in it, which gives you an easy place to start cutting out the circle.

3. Cut out the shape of the circle through both sides of the envelope. Ask for help if you need it. Now your envelope should have a round hole in the middle of it.

4. Open the envelope and slide the piece of cellophane into it. Close the envelope and seal it to keep the cellophane in place. (If the cellophane slides around, you can tape it on the inside of the envelope before sealing it.)

5. Decorate your envelope however you like.

6. Now look through your viewfinder! Notice how the world looks now!

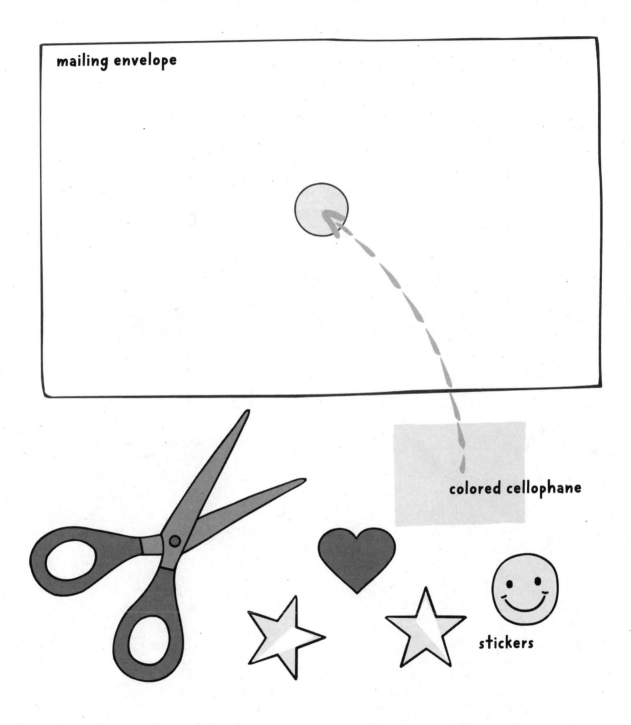

Finding Your Superhero

In the first part of this chapter, you learned about the inner bully, a worthy but challenging part of yourself. Here's the best part—a superhero lives inside you, too. This part of you can be supportive and kind and has strengths that you can use when you need them the most. Your superhero lets you know that you are not alone when things get tough. This part of yourself is waiting to be discovered!

Can you name some of the strengths and superpowers of your superhero?

Color in the POW symbol next to the superpowers you would like your superhero to have:

SUPERHERO CHECKLIST

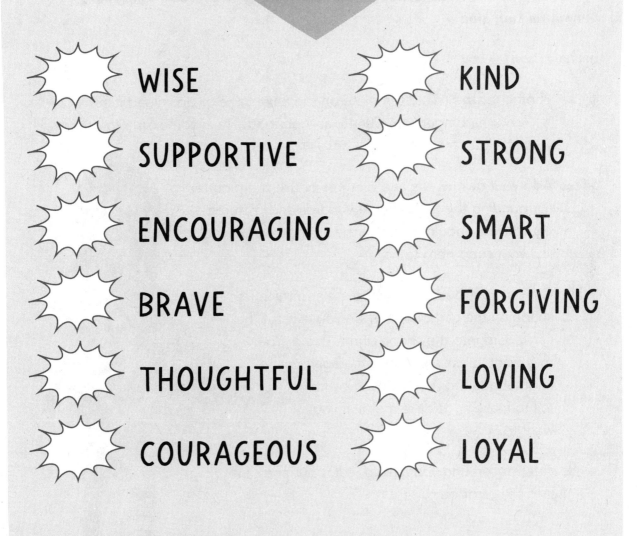

WISE

SUPPORTIVE

ENCOURAGING

BRAVE

THOUGHTFUL

COURAGEOUS

KIND

STRONG

SMART

FORGIVING

LOVING

LOYAL

Making a Superhero Shield

Now you can design your own superhero shield with words that describe the strengths of your superhero.

Materials you will need: scissors, marker or crayons, piece of cardboard, aluminum foil, glue

Instructions:

1. Photocopy the shield template on the next page or download it at http://www.newharbinger.com/50645, and print out. Take some time to decorate your shield.

2. Add your own words and pictures or use the pictures surrounding the template. The words and pictures you choose should describe the strengths you would like your superhero to have.

3. Cut out your decorated template and trace its shape on the cardboard. Then you can cut the cardboard into the shape of the shield. You may want to ask a parent or caregiver or another adult for help. Cover it with foil to make it look like metal, if you want to.

4. After decorating your shield, cut it out and glue it to the cardboard.

What Does Your Superhero Have to Say?

Your superhero has supportive things to say to you when you are having difficulty. Here are some things your superhero may say. **Choose one from the list or think of your own and put it in the speech bubble.**

- *Sorry things are so tough right now.*

- *They'll get better. Just hang in there.*

- *It'll be okay.*

- *I want you to know I'm here for you.*

- *You have what it takes to make a change!*

- *You've got this.*

Revealing Your Superhero

So what does your inner superhero look like? You might imagine them as a person, an animal, or a comic book character. Sketch your superhero to show how strong, large, or powerful you want them to be.

Draw your inner superhero here:

#1 LOVE SUPERHEROES WITH A KIND HEART!

Compassionate Superhero Meditation

A superhero can also be a great and compassionate friend. After naming the unique qualities of your superhero and deciding what you would like to hear from them, you can imagine how they can encourage you through a challenging time. Start with this meditation on your compassionate inner superhero.

1. Get into a comfortable position. You can lie down if you wish. You might close your eyes and begin to feel your breath, just noticing your breath coming and going.

2. Now, see if you can think about a time when you were upset, not the worst time but something that was just a little upsetting to you. For example, someone called you a name at school, or maybe you felt left out, or your sibling got you into trouble for something you didn't do.

3. Think about this situation as clearly as you can. Who was there? What was said?

4. Can you pay attention to what feelings are here now? Or what about your body? Does it want to get up and move or lie still? Does it feel relaxed or tight and tense?

5. Now imagine your superhero coming to help you in this difficult moment.

6. What might your superhero say to you that would be kind and comforting? See if you can remember what words you would like your superhero to say to comfort you, words like *It's going to be okay* or *I care about you.*

7. What would your superhero do to help take care of you right now? Do you need a hug or do you need your superhero to stand up for you in some way? Can you imagine your superhero taking care of you right now?

8. Can you pay attention to how it feels to know that your special friend, your superhero, has got your back?

9. Take a few last breaths and allow yourself to enjoy the good feeling of meeting your superhero, knowing your superhero is always there whenever you need them.

10. Now, gently open your eyes.

What a great job you've done! The important thing to remember is that your superhero is a part of you. This kind and compassionate part of you is there to teach you to be good to yourself when you are struggling.

One way to take good care of yourself is by knowing about your superhero's brave and courageous heart!

ACTIVITY
53

Superhero Yoga Pose

The kind heart is also a brave heart. It can fight for what is right and say no to things that are wrong, like when a bully is pushing you around.

This pose can help you feel the strength of your superhero and remind you of your fierce and protective side.

1. Stand up strong and tall with your hands on your hips and with your feet slightly apart, like a superhero would stand.

2. Then, inhale and jump your feet apart, so your legs create a big triangle with the ground. Stretch your arms straight out to the sides as high as your shoulders.

3. Turn both feet to the right.

4. Don't forget to breathe!

5. Bend your front leg to a right angle, keeping your back leg straight.

6. Keep your arms straight.

7. After one or two breaths, inhale and straighten your front leg and turn both feet forward again, while placing your hands on your waist. See if you can feel the strength of your superhero.

8. Now, repeat steps 2 through 7 but switching in step 3 to the left side.

9. Now jump your feet together to stand tall for three full breaths.

10. Pay attention to your body and your breath. You are strong and powerful...just like a superhero.

Remember that you can stand up for yourself with the help of your superhero. Also remember this strong side of your superhero knows to ask for help from an adult who can support you.

Building Your Toolkit

You have now investigated your inner bully and your superhero, so you'll be able to recognize these two parts of yourself when they show up. Doing the activities in this chapter strengthens your superhero.

What are some things you can do when your inner bully shows up? Check off the activities that you believe can support you.

___ Getting to Know Your Inner Bully

___ Getting the Inner Bully Out of Your Head

___ Three Soothing Breaths

___ A New Way of Seeing

___ Viewfinder for Seeing Things in a New Way

___ Finding Your Superhero

___ Making a Superhero Shield

___ Revealing Your Superhero

___ Compassionate Superhero Meditation

___ Superhero Yoga Pose

SHARING IS CARING

What activities or ideas about the inner superhero would you like to share with a friend? Write a friend's name and an activity or idea that you would like to share.

Your friend's name: _____

What would you like to share with them? _____

_____

_____

TO BE REVEALED

In the next chapter, you will investigate the mystery of how your core values guide you to safety in difficult times. You will discover how to be strong and stick with what matters most to you.

What Matters Most to You

Have you ever wondered what makes you *you*? What you care about and the things you believe in are what help to make you the special and unique person you are. These are called *core values*. In this chapter, you will get to explore your core values and maybe consider how these values connect you with others. Core values point you in the direction you want to go. They help to shape the kind of person you are becoming. Think about what makes you happy or the things that interest you, like being a good friend or doing your best in school or in sports. How you spend your free time is one way of understanding what matters most to you, and it helps others to see who you are.

Core values help to build character, strength, and resilience. They're like an inner compass that keeps you headed in the right direction. Core values can also be like the roots of a tree that help you stay upright and make good decisions, especially when things are stormy and difficult. Sometimes, there are obstacles that can keep you from living your core values in the way that you want. For example, you may love to be outdoors, but you live in a really cold climate, so your time outside is limited by the weather, or you love sports, but you have a physical condition that prevents you from playing the way you would like. It's times like this that self-compassion can be a good core value to have in your toolkit.

How Do You Like to Spend Your Time?

One way to figure out what matters to you is to look at what you do each day. Here is a chance to show how you spend your time. The pie slices below will help you illustrate the types of things you do each day.

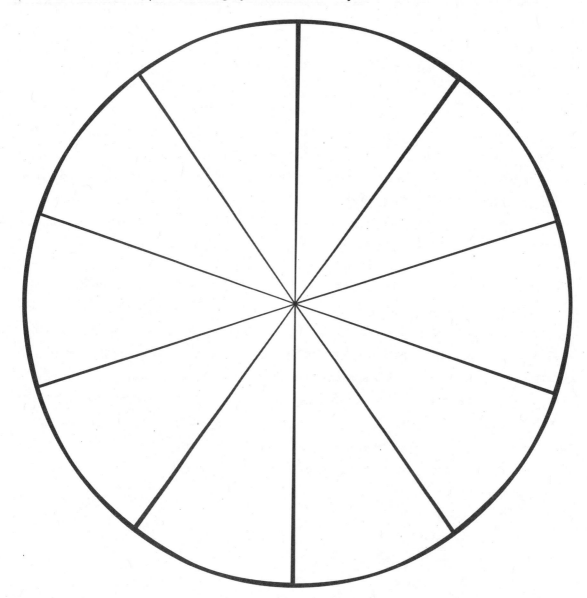

Use your crayons or markers to color in the slices to show how much time you spend doing activities that are important to you. For example, if you spend a lot of time playing sports, you could color in the whole sports pie slice. Or if you only play a little sports each week, you could just color in a little of the pie slice. You can choose a different color for each slice of pie or you can choose one color for the whole pie.

What do you spend the most time doing?

_____

Is this something that is important to you? Circle your answer: YES   NO

Is there something you would like to spend more time doing? If so, please describe what it is:

_____

_____

_____

Write down one thing that keeps you from doing what is important to you:

_____

_____

Remember to give yourself a little kindness or self-compassion when you can't do something that is important to you.

Discovering Your Core Values

Your core values determine how you will grow. For example, if helping others is very important to you, then you will grow to be a helpful person.

Knowing your core values is a good way to know what really matters to you. **To discover your own core values, read through this list of values, and put a check mark next to any that are important to you:**

☐ Getting good grades

☐ Being good in sports

☐ Being attractive

☐ Being neat and tidy

☐ Being the best at everything

☐ Enjoying time in nature

☐ Sharing

☐ Being a good friend

☐ Being kind

☐ Helping others

☐ Being creative

☐ Expressing yourself

☐ Playing and having fun

☐ Being popular

☐ Being rich

☐ Being famous

☐ Spending time with your family

☐ Spending time with friends

☐ Your religion or faith

☐ Being honest

☐ Getting to be yourself

☐ Trying new things

☐ Having quiet time to yourself

☐ Learning new things

☐ Doing your hobbies

☐ Working hard

☐ Being thankful

☐ Being happy

☐ Taking care of the environment

☐ Being safe

☐ Having courage

☐ Standing up for what is right

☐ Is there another value that's important to you? Write it down here.

_____

Review the values that you checked off, and circle your top five favorites. Include any that you wrote down that weren't on the list. The values that you circle are your core values, or the values that matter to you most.

As you may know, trees grow from their roots on up. Use the tree picture to see how you will grow. **Write your top five values in the tree roots and color in your tree with crayons or markers any way you wish.**

ACTIVITY 56

Exploring Nature

In Japan, there is a practice called *forest bathing*. This is a special way of walking in nature and being awake to all the sights and sounds with appreciation. Just being in nature can calm and soothe you, especially when you are paying attention to it. In this reflection, see if you can be aware of how your senses might react to your environment.

Choose a place to walk with permission from your parent or caregiver where you can be surrounded by nature. As you walk, open your eyes wide to help you see, open your ears to help you hear, and let your nose pick up all of the different smells of nature. Stop from time to time to focus on what your senses pick up. Nature is a core value shared by people in many cultures around the world. See if you can discover how nature supports your core values, for example, noticing how nature allows you to be with friends outdoors, if friendship is a core value.

When you finish your walk, come back to draw what you discovered. You may even choose to bring something back with you to draw on your page.

"A Tree and Me" Meditation

One way to be with nature is to use your imagination. In this activity, you will imagine sitting with your back against a tree and allowing yourself to feel the strength and stability of this towering giant. Trees are resilient and can weather storms and give support to other trees who need help!

1. Take a moment to find a comfortable position.

2. When you feel ready, gently close your eyes or look down at your knees.

3. Now, take a few deep breaths…in and out, and then let your breathing be gentle and easy.

4. Be sure to notice when your puppy mind is wandering and bring it back to your breath.

5. Now imagine yourself sitting underneath a large tree, resting comfortably.

6. Take a moment to imagine how solid and stable this tree is. Let yourself feel the strength of this tree as you rest underneath it, noticing how this particular tree stretches upward toward the sky with its many branches.

7. Now, imagine the roots of the tree, connecting them to the earth and to the other trees around. Trees have a root system that allows them to support one another and care for one another.

8. Imagine yourself also as a tree with roots growing deep into the earth and your back as a strong, solid trunk that supports you and allows you to stand firm in stormy weather.

9. Remember that your core values can keep you rooted to what is important in your life and allow you to care for yourself and others when needed.

10. Rest comfortably for a few breaths and when you are ready, gently open your eyes.

Circle the emoji that shows how you feel after imagining yourself as a strong and stable tree rooted to the earth.

"Being a Tree" Yoga Pose

What would it be like to feel the strength and stability of a tree in your own body? In this yoga pose, you can imagine that you are growing roots through your feet deep into the earth and using your arms like branches of a tree, stretching upward toward the sky.

This pose is great for balancing and improving concentration. You can feel the strength and stability of a tree in your body, just as your core values keep you focused and rooted in what matters most in your life. See if you can hold the pose and feel quiet in your mind.

1. Begin by standing strong and stable like a mountain with your feet together.

2. Look straight ahead at something out in front of you, but with only a soft focus. You can imagine you are gazing out through a forest of trees. Keep staring at that spot throughout the practice. You can tell yourself, *I believe in myself and what matters to me*, as you move through this pose.

3. Place your hands on your waist as you inhale and bend your right knee, turn it out to the side, and place the sole of your right foot on the inside of your left calf, or just rest the heel of your right foot on your left ankle. Breathe in and breathe out.

4. Keep your left leg firm, strong like the trunk of a tree.

5. Imagine your left leg growing roots deep into the earth to help you feel steady.

6. Inhale again and press your right foot into your left leg, so you feel like your legs are the trunk of the tree. You might notice how strong your trunk feels. Breathe in and breathe out.

7. If you can, bring the palms of your hands together in front of your heart. Pause for a moment and, then as you inhale, lift your arms overhead with your hands apart.

8. Keep your arms reaching upward, then imagine roots growing deep into the earth from your left foot. Just as this Tree pose helps you feel strong and stable in your body, your core values can help you feel strong and stable in your life.

9. When you are ready to switch sides, turn your right knee to the front, exhale and slowly lower your hands to your chest and your foot to the floor.

10. Then practice Tree pose with your other leg.

How did it go? If you find you need some support balancing, you can use a chair to hold onto, or rest against a wall until you feel like you can balance on your own.

Your Body Map

This activity is a fun way to get to see how your core values help you take the actions in your body that you want to take. You can create a body map that shows how your favorite core values move you.

Read the following questions for each part of your body, and write your answers on the corresponding part of the body outline.

Your hair: What skills or attitudes would you like to grow in your life? Friendliness, uniqueness, humor, kindness, toughness, gentleness, attractiveness, or something else?

Your eyes: What is important for you to see when you look in the mirror? Your confidence, strength, creativity, beauty, silliness, goodness, or something else?

Your ears: What is important for you to hear? Sounds of nature, praise from teachers or parents for doing a good job, good news about someone's health or safety, laughter from friends, or something else?

Your mouth: How do you want to talk to others? With humor, honesty, bravery, kindness, toughness, or something else?

Your arms: Whom would you like to stay connected to? A family member, a friend, a hero, a pet, a coach, a spiritual leader, or a special community? Or is there someone you would like to reach out to?

Your hands: What would you like to create with your hands? A craft, beautiful music, a story, a winning catch, a hairstyle, a thank-you note, a more organized room, or something else?

Your legs: What do you want to stand up for? Kids who are being bullied, clean air or water, your right to speak your mind, your privacy, the truth, or something else?

Your feet: Where do you want your feet to take you now and in your life? To your school, your friend's house, the park or playground, the library, or a store, or on a new adventure? Or somewhere else?

If you like, you can sit down with a parent, a caregiver, or a friend and share your core values to help them understand who you are and who you want to be. Remember that core values can help you create a kind attitude toward yourself and all living beings.

A Promise Just for You

After you've decorated your picture frame, choose one core value that can guide you to becoming the person you want to be. See if you can turn this core value into a promise for yourself.

Decorate the outside frame with whatever colors and designs you like.

This promise can be like a safe place to return to when you feel a little lost. An example might be, "I wish to be a good friend" or "I wish to take good care of myself" or maybe "I wish to put more effort into my schoolwork." **Write your promise inside the frame.**

If you like, you can cut out this picture frame and pin it to your wall just to remind yourself of your promise. Ask a parent or caregiver or another adult if you need help.

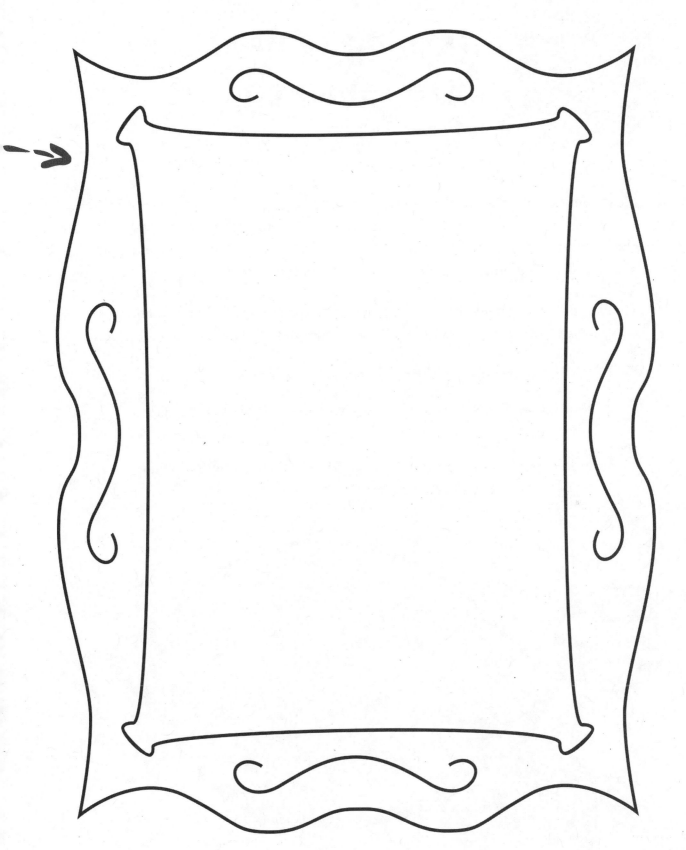

123

ACTIVITY
61

Turning Lemons into Lemonade

Most everyone is afraid to fail! But it is the mistakes or snafus in life that can teach us the most important lessons. That's because when you struggle, you have a chance to discover strengths you didn't know you had. This can make you sturdier and more resilient and will help you recover from difficulty more quickly.

Think of a time when you had a struggle or made a mistake, maybe a time when you worked hard on something, but it didn't turn out the way you wanted it to.

1. Write the struggle or the sour situation in the lemon drawing below.

2. Write down the lesson you learned from that mistake on the glass of lemonade.

3. Now write on the straw in the glass the core values that might have helped you in this situation.

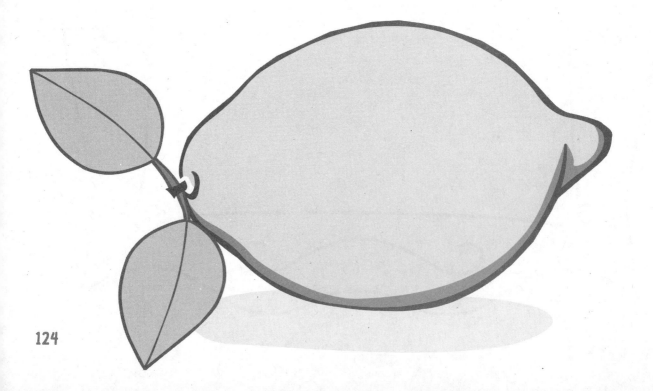

This activity shows how you turned lemons into lemonade, which is turning a sour situation into a sweet one.

Homemade Lemonade

Making your own lemonade is a way to remind yourself that you can often turn a sour situation into a sweet one by looking for the way it strengthened you.

Homemade Lemonade Recipe

Ingredients

1 1/2 cups freshly squeezed lemon juice (you can use the bottled juice too)

5 cups cold water

1 1/2 cups sugar or a sweetener alternative like stevia (start with 1 teaspoon and sweeten to taste)

Ice

Step 1 Combine lemon juice, water, and sugar into a large pitcher and stir until sugar is completely dissolved.

Step 2 Top with ice to keep it nice and cold.

Be sure to use your mindfulness skills as you prepare your lemonade and then savor and enjoy with all of your senses.

Building Your Toolkit

Now that you've learned what core values are, you can depend on them to help guide you in the direction you want to go and to help you be who you want to be.

Put a check mark next to the activities you learned in this chapter that you would like to try again:

___ How Do You Like to Spend Your Time?

___ Discovering Your Core Values

___ Exploring Nature

___ "A Tree and Me" Meditation

___ "Being a Tree" Yoga Pose

___ Your Body Map

___ A Promise Just for You

___ Turning Lemons into Lemonade

___ Homemade Lemonade

 ## SHARING IS CARING

What have you learned about core values that you would like to share with a friend? Write a friend's name and an activity or idea that you would like to share:

Your friend's name: _____

What would you like to share with them? _____

_____

TO BE REVEALED

In the next chapter, you will discover for yourself how to work with strong emotions that can sometimes take you by surprise. Recognizing what you can do to keep your upstairs brain and downstairs brain connected can keep you on track and connected to yourself and others with more kindness and compassion.

CHAPTER 7

How to Tame Your Inner Dragon

Everyone, no matter their age, experiences big emotions. Some of these big emotions can feel good, such as joy and excitement, but sometimes they can feel scary, like there is a fire-breathing dragon living inside you. When things go wrong, you might feel like you can't handle these big emotions. In this chapter, you will learn where these big and sometimes scary emotions come from and how to tame and befriend them. You can begin this journey by getting to know what some of these emotions are and how to meet them with a brave heart. Once you know how to meet them, you will learn how to tame them just like a dragon rider knows how to tame a fire-breathing dragon.

ACTIVITY 63

Meeting Your Big Emotions with a Brave Heart

Look at the expressions below and circle the big emotions that you have ever felt.

Frustration

Disappointment

Sadness

Scared

Anger

Now, write the emotion that is the biggest challenge for you and that you would like to get to know better.

Dragon's Breath Yoga Pose

Have you ever heard a dragon roar? It can be loud and sometimes fiery. Maybe you've heard your own inner dragon from time to time. In this yoga pose, you use a powerful dragon's breath to tame your inner dragon.

1. Imagine a fire-breathing dragon as you stand on both feet about hip width apart. Raise your hands up to your chest and bend your fingers to make claws.

2. Now, take a deep breath in, and as you breathe out, open your mouth wide, stick out your tongue as far as you can, and make a big loud roar like a dragon.

3. Repeat deep breathing in and roaring as your breathe out several more times. As you breathe in, lift your head up and back like a dragon getting ready to breathe out a fiery roar, and stretch your tongue out as you roar out your next breath.

4. Notice how it feels to breathe out like a dragon.

The next time you notice your inner dragon of big feelings boiling up inside you, you can do this dragon's breath to blow it all out with the fiery roar of a dragon.

MORE

What happened in your body when you breathed out and roared like a dragon? Circle the words that describe how you felt in your body.

warmth	energy
excitement	relaxation
strength	coolness
tiredness	tightness

Did you notice some other emotions that came up when you breathed like a dragon? Like silly or calm?

WHERE THE INNER DRAGON LIVES

One way to understand your brain is to think of it like a house with an upstairs and a downstairs (Siegel and Payne Bryson 2012). The upstairs and downstairs are two parts of the brain that work together to help you manage big emotions and to make good decisions.

Here's a little more about the two parts of the brain. See if you can guess where the inner dragon lives.

The job of your *upstairs brain* is to help you solve problems and make good decisions. It is also responsible for helping you focus your attention and to help you calm yourself down. The prefrontal cortex (PFC) is a special part of the upstairs brain that helps the upstairs and downstairs brain work together. One way to think about your PFC is that it is like a *dragon rider*, who can guide and tame your inner dragon with all of those big emotions.

You need the *downstairs brain* because it protects you from dangerous or scary situations that sound the alarm in a little place called the amygdala. When this alarm goes off, it wakes up your big emotions. Sometimes these emotions can feel like a fire-breathing dragon that jumps into action when it hears the alarm. Sometimes this inner dragon gets carried away and can react in ways that you might feel bad about, like saying mean things to others.

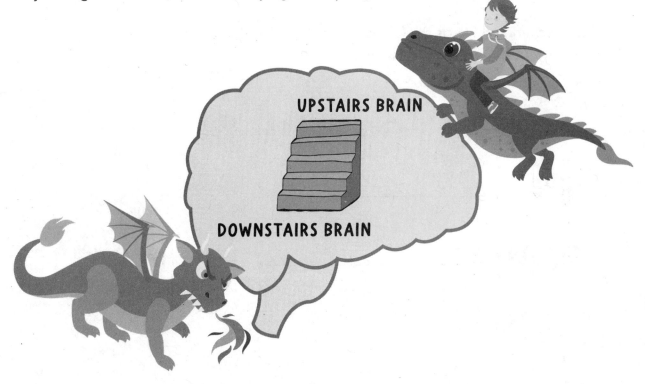

UPSTAIRS BRAIN

DOWNSTAIRS BRAIN

When the upstairs and downstairs brain are communicating, you feel in control and safe. You can make good decisions, handle challenges, and feel good about yourself and others. It's like having a dragon rider that knows how to train and tame the inner dragon.

To manage your emotions, it helps for the upstairs and downstairs brain to stay connected, just as a staircase connects the upstairs and downstairs in a house. The good news is you can learn to give your dragon rider tools to tame your inner dragon and to soothe your big emotions. This will let your dragon rider go downstairs to work with your dragon, so you can stay calm and in control. In a moment, you can learn more ways to build your staircase, but first you can try this fun activity to review what you've learned about your brain.

Unscramble Your Brain

These scrambled words are words about the brain that you have just learned.
See if you can unscramble them.

AINRB _____

GALMDAAY _____

PURTAISS _____

CPF _____

ASTRISWNDO _____

NGDARO _____

Answers: brain, amygdala, upstairs, PFC, downstairs, dragon

ACTIVITY
66

The Magic of Oobleck

Oobleck is a magical and fun way to learn how your big emotions can melt away when you are kind and compassionate with yourself. You will use your mindfulness skills to explore the surprising qualities in this mysterious substance. See if you can discover the secret of what makes the Oobleck hard and what makes it soften or melt.

Materials you will need: large bowl, measuring cup, spoon, box of cornstarch, food coloring, glitter, water

Instructions:

To make the Oobleck, measure one cup of water and one and a half cups of cornstarch. Mix together in a bowl with a spoon or with your hands. If it won't hold a solid shape when you squeeze it, work in more cornstarch a few tablespoons at a time until it's the right consistency. It will take a few minutes of mixing to get just right. If you like, add a few drops of food coloring and a few shakes of glitter. Continue to mix and add more food coloring and glitter, little by little, to your liking.

MORE

1. Now take some time to just feel the Oobleck in your hands.

2. Notice how the texture of the Oobleck feels.

3. Notice what happens when you squeeze it tightly in one hand and how it changes shape from being soft and liquidy to firm and solid as you squeeze it.

4. Notice what happens when you open your hand again.

5. After washing your hands, write down below what you discovered about the mystery of Oobleck. What happened when you gripped the Oobleck tightly and what happened when you opened your hand?

Write down what you discovered as you worked with the Oobleck.

_____

_____

_____

You probably noticed how the Oobleck hardened when you squeezed it in your hand and it softened again when you opened your hand and let it go. Big emotions are the same. Sometimes when your inner dragon takes control, big emotions can make your body feel tight and squeezed. But when you relax and breathe and let go, the body can soften and these big emotions can melt away.

In the next couple of activities, you will have a chance to name a strong emotion and find where it shows up in your body. Then you will have a chance to soften and let go of the strong emotion just like you did with the Oobleck.

A "Name It to Tame It" Exercise

This idea of naming our emotions to help tame them comes from a book by Dan Siegel and Tina Payne Bryson (2012). It's all about naming your big emotion. When you name a big emotion, that helps to tame it. This is because using the upstairs brain to name an emotion helps connect it to your downstairs brain, so they can work together better and help you stay in charge. The time to do this exercise is when big emotions show up and feel like they are about to take over.

See if you can remember a time when you felt angry, fearful, lonely, sad, or worried. Try not to use the biggest emotion, but choose something easy since you are just learning. **Write down the situation that you remember.**

_____

_____

Name one of the feelings you notice as you recall the memory. You might name the emotion by saying, "This is sadness," "This is anger," or "This is worry."

Circle the emoji below that shows the emotion you named in this practice.

| Anger | Fear | Loneliness | Sadness | Worry |

Naming your big emotions when they show up can help your dragon rider begin to tame your inner dragon.

Finding the Emotion in Your Body

Naming an emotion helps to tame the dragon. It also helps to find where the emotion shows up in your body, so you can soothe yourself. When your inner dragon gets upset, often the first sign is that you start to feel things in your body, like tightness, butterflies in the stomach, sweaty palms, or even a headache.

Now recall the big emotion you felt in the "Name It to Tame It" exercise you just completed. When you feel that big emotion, what happens in your body? You can zero in on the emotion in your body if you look for it.

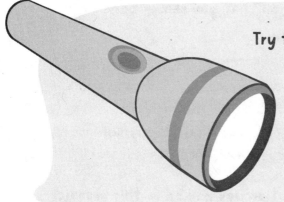

Try this: Imagine you have a flashlight and you are shining it on your body from head to toe to see where the big emotion is showing up in your body. Maybe you will find a tense muscle, butterflies in your stomach, or a tightness in your hands or chest.

In the image on the next page, use markers or crayons to color all the areas where you notice any sensations in your body. You can show how strong the sensation is by how much of the body you color. You can also choose colors that help show what it feels like. Feel free to add shapes or words to show how your body feels or what it does when this big emotion shows up.

"Soften, Soothe, and Let It Be" Meditation

In this activity, you can learn to soften the big emotions in the body just like you did with the Oobleck. Choose just one achy or tense spot in your body that needs some attention from the last activity. This might be the place where the emotion you named is hiding.

1. Sit comfortably or lie down and close your eyes.

2. Bring attention to the achy or tense spot in your body that needs some attention now.

3. Now *soften* the tightness or achy feeling in this spot. Send a kind breath to it and imagine kindness helping to melt it just like an ice cube in the sun.

4. *Soothe* this ache or uncomfortable feeling by putting your hand over your heart and feeling your body breathe. Maybe even give yourself some kind words, such as *It will be okay* or *I'm doing my best.*

It will be okay

5. *Let it be.* Sometimes things don't change as quickly as you might want them to. See if you can be with how things are right now as you continue to send kind wishes to yourself and your muscles begin to relax and let go.

6. You may gently open your eyes.

If you find this meditation helpful, you can do it anywhere, anytime. You can do it sitting in your classroom or sitting with friends. Just notice any strong emotion that comes up and first name it. Then, see if you can find it in your body, and begin to soften, soothe, and let it be. If you remember how the Oobleck felt in your hand as you opened it, this is kind of what happens when you soften and soothe your big emotions in your body.

I'm doing my best

Taking Your Dragon for a Walk

When was the last time you took a walk in the forest or in a park? Nature has so many things to teach you and can be a great way to soothe yourself. You can even take your dragon for a walk, especially when you're having a hard time. One way to do this is to let all the amazing things nature has to offer wake up your senses.

After getting permission from your parent or caregiver, give yourself at least ten to fifteen minutes to take a walk in a park, a forest, or even down your street. You can also walk in your own backyard. Nature is everywhere!

1. Before you begin your walk, stand still with your eyes closed.

2. When you open your eyes, allow yourself to take in all of the colors, shapes, and textures of everything around you.

3. After walking for a few moments, you can stop and close your eyes again, listening to all the sounds around you and even noticing the smells.

4. Now open your eyes and continue walking and, when you're ready, stop to touch a leaf, the ground, or even the bark of a tree.

5. If you like, you can taste something a parent or caregiver has told you is safe to taste. Be wise about what you're willing to taste.

6. When you return from your walk, draw a picture of one thing that was interesting or pleasant to you…and your dragon!

Draw here

A Friendly Sock Snake to Soothe You

Another way to soothe your inner dragon with its big emotions is with a gentle, warm touch. In this case, you'll make a sock snake, warm it up, and put it on the part of your body that needs some comfort.

Materials you will need: a clean knee-length sock, rice, nontoxic fabric markers, an essential oil such as lavender (optional)

Instructions:

1. Take the sock and fill it three-fourths of the way with rice. If you would like to add a soothing scent, you can add a few drops of essential oil to the rice.

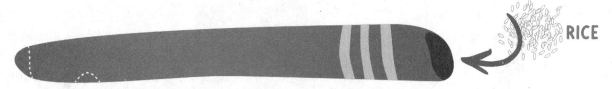

RICE

2. Tie a knot in the end to close it up.

3. Use fabric markers to decorate it and draw a snake face (eyes, mouth, and forked tongue) at the end of the sock that does not have a knot.

4. Now you have made a sock snake that you can use to soothe sore muscles. Simply heat your sock snake in a microwave, thirty seconds at a time, until it is warm but not hot. Make sure that you have a parent or caregiver help you with this step.

5. Use your sock snake to relax and soften any part of your body that feels sore or tight. You might even close your eyes and take a few deep breaths while you enjoy this soothing experience. Breath in and make a hissing sound as you exhale, if you like, to sound like a snake.

Your Calm and Resting Inner Dragon

Color your dragon now that you've learned how to soothe it.

Building Your Toolkit

Congratulations! You have now learned some good ways to tame your inner dragon, so your big emotions can be less scary and can even feel useful by alerting you to danger.

What are some ways your dragon rider can quiet your big emotions? Check off the ones that you want to try:

___ Meeting Your Big Emotions with a Brave Heart

___ Dragon's Breath Yoga Pose

___ Unscramble Your Brain

___ The Magic of Oobleck

___ "A Name It to Tame It" Exercise

___ Finding the Emotion in Your Body

___ "Soften, Soothe, and Let It Be" Meditation

___ Taking Your Dragon for a Walk

___ A Friendly Sock Snake to Soothe You

___ Your Calm and Resting Inner Dragon

 ## SHARING IS CARING

What have you learned about the inner dragon that you would like to share with a friend? Write a friend's name and the activity or idea that you would like to share:

Your friend's name: _____

What would you like to share with them? _____

_____

TO BE REVEALED

This next chapter will help you discover how to grow positive emotions and attitudes like gratitude, a way to be thankful, which can also help you handle strong emotions.

CHAPTER 8

Gratitude Makes You Happy

When you were very little, you may remember your parents or caregivers telling you to say thank you when you received a gift. This is a way of showing appreciation and gratitude for a nice gesture. When you show appreciation for something or someone, or when you have gratitude for all the little things in your life, it can help you feel happy, joyful, and even more confident. Being grateful can actually help you feel more generous toward others, too, maybe those who have helped you achieve something important. After all, gratitude is a positive feeling, so it connects you to your heart space and makes room for more joy!

In this chapter, you will be able to recognize the many things in your life you are grateful for, big and small. And you will get a chance to experience the benefits of gratitude and appreciation, especially for yourself. Gratitude and appreciation are connected to skills you've learned in this workbook: kindness, empathy, compassion, resilience, and emotional strength. Gratitude is another superpower that helps you see your own good qualities and the good qualities in others. This superpower is especially helpful when things feel like a struggle in some way. You can always find something to be grateful for, and this can make a difference in how you see things in the moment!

Six Islands of Gratitude

Explore the six islands of gratitude on the map to discover what you are truly grateful for. Each island has its own name, which gives a clue to what you truly appreciate in your life.

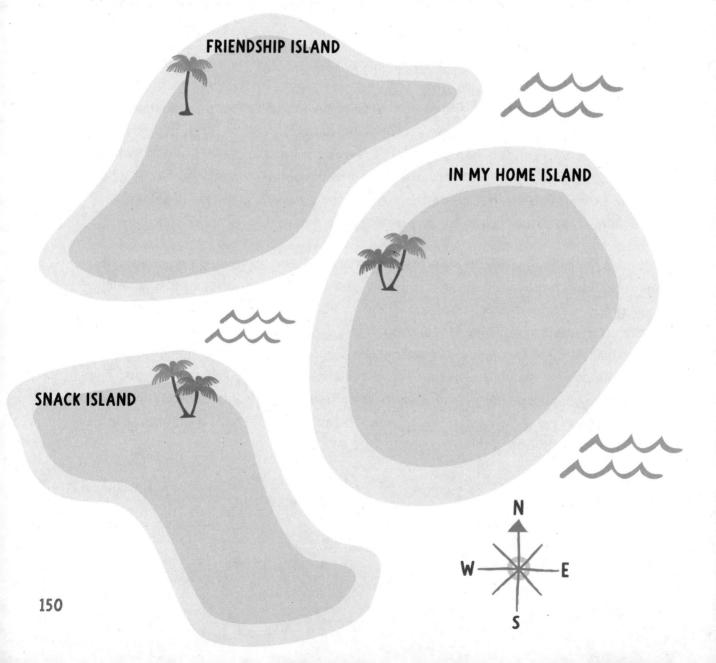

FRIENDSHIP ISLAND

IN MY HOME ISLAND

SNACK ISLAND

What are you grateful for? Take a moment to think about six things big and small that bring you joy and make you happy. **Write these things on the islands where they belong.**

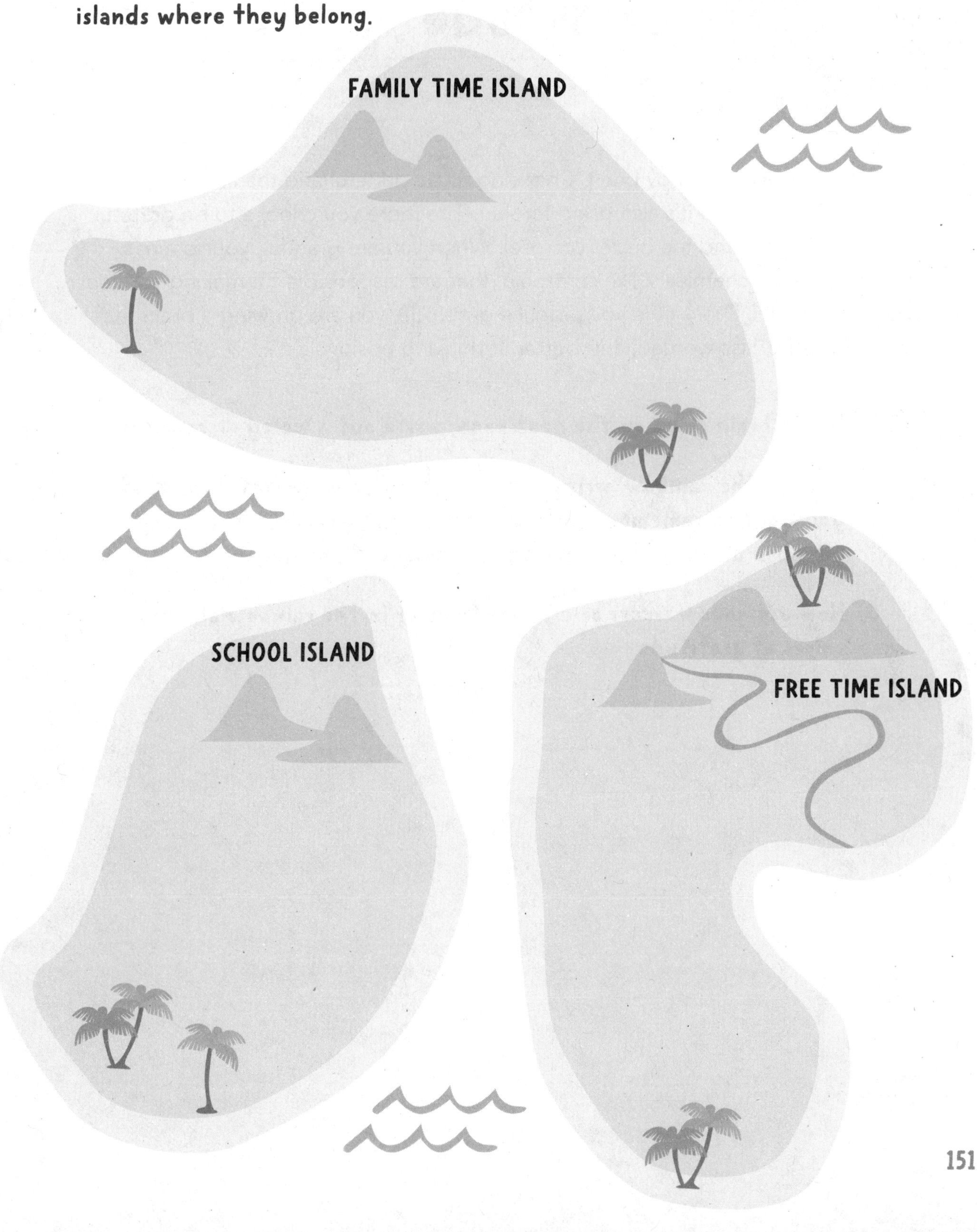

FAMILY TIME ISLAND

SCHOOL ISLAND

FREE TIME ISLAND

Your Brain on Gratitude

A grateful brain is a happy brain. Choosing to be grateful and thank others is a kind thing to do, and it's also good for you. The more you choose to be grateful, the easier it gets and the better you feel. When you are grateful, your brain releases special chemicals, like serotonin, that are responsible for making you feel good and joyful. Every time you practice gratitude, you are growing a brain that is more happy, less worried, and better at thinking positively.

1. **In the brain cloud on the next page, write out a worry or concern.**

2. **Then in the rainbow, write out something to be grateful for that you want to remember when you have that worry.** Even if you can't get rid of the worry, you can build a happier brain to hold it.

3. **Now use your markers or crayons to color in the rainbow all the colors of gratitude.**

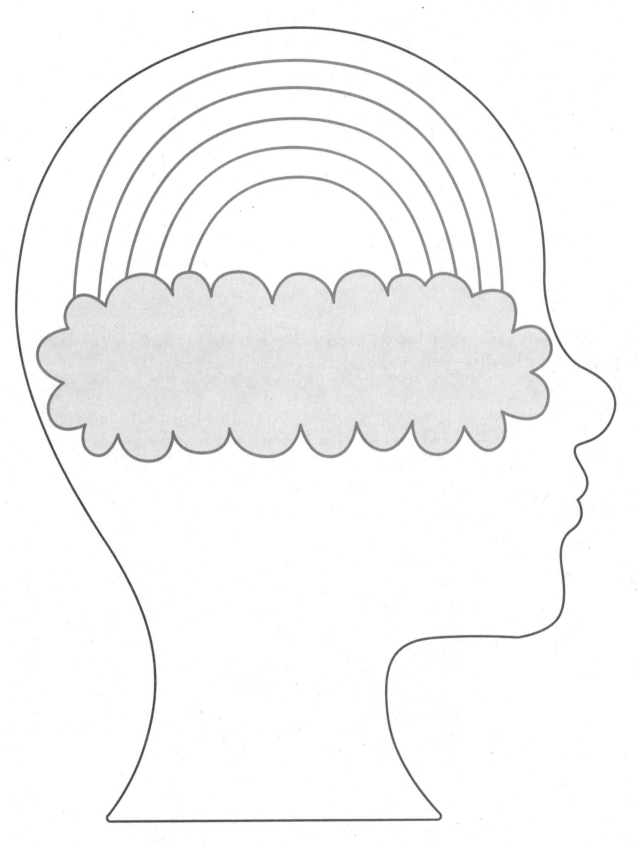

"Thank You from Me to a Bee"

Another way to grow your gratitude is to mindfully pay attention to the world around you. With the help of a grown-up, find a place outdoors to wander around in. It could be a park, your backyard, a trail at a park, or someplace else. Open up your senses to what you can see, hear, feel, and smell, and perhaps even taste, to find one thing that you are grateful for.

(And while you are out there, pick up a stick and bring it back for the next activity. The stick should be about two pencils long.)

Once you are back from wandering around, **write a thank-you note to the part of nature that fills your heart with gratitude.** For example, you might write to the sun for warming you, the grass for giving you a soft place to walk, a rain puddle for giving you something fun to jump in, or a tree for giving you a stick to play with. Sign the letter with your name at the end.

Dear _____,

Thank you for _____.

It made me feel _____.

It's good to know that you are part of my world.

Yours truly,

_____

Gratitude Stick

Whenever you practice gratitude, your brain gets better at creating positive thoughts and feelings, so it's good to have something to remind you to practice it. In this case, you can make a gratitude stick.

Materials you will need: stick (about two pencils long), several pieces of yarn (or thin strips of fabric), beads to attach to the yarn, scissors

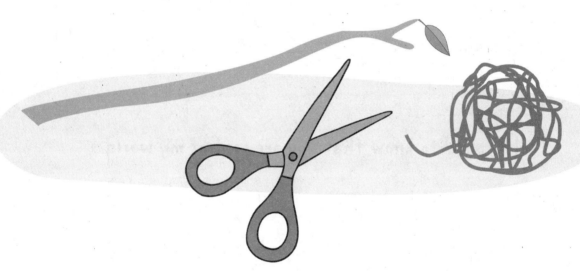

Instructions:

1. Cut your yarn to about three feet long. Ask a parent or caregiver or another adult for help if you need it.

2. Tightly tie one end of the yarn to one end of the stick.

3. Add beads to the yarn and any other items you like for decoration, and then make a knot at the end.

4. Now wrap the yarn all the way down the stick. When you're finished, tie the end of the yarn to the stick and make a knot. Repeat, using as many pieces of yarn as you like to decorate the stick.

Now you have made a gratitude stick. Put it somewhere you will see it often to remind you to pick it up and name something you are grateful for.

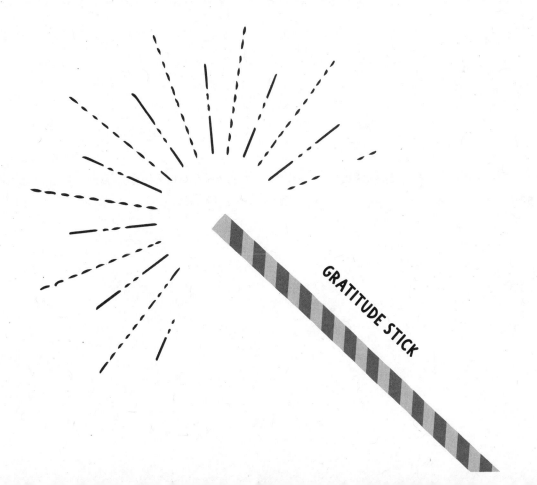

GRATITUDE STICK

ACTIVITY 77

"Thanks to the Many Hands That Feed Me"

Everything you need to nourish your body is grown somewhere on the planet by a farmer, but the farmer can't do it all alone. The foods that you enjoy eating every day need help from other resources too, like water, soil, wind, and sun. In this activity, you can show gratitude to everything that nourishes you to help you stay healthy and strong. To begin, grab one of your favorite foods from the kitchen.

Now, as you prepare to eat this delicious treat, remember to use all your senses to help you enjoy it: sight, touch, smell, taste, and even hearing. You might notice the colors, shape, or aroma of the food.

Write some words of appreciation for the earth and all of the elements involved in growing this food, like water, the sun, the wind, and the soil.

_____

_____

_____

Write words of appreciation to all the friends involved in growing, picking, packaging, and transporting your favorite foods.

_____

_____

_____

Write just a few words of appreciation to your parents or caregivers for providing you with this favorite food.

_____

_____

Now, take a moment to write down a few words of appreciation for the food that nourishes your body and for your body for all of the ways it helps to keep you healthy!

_____

_____

If you like, you can also express your appreciation by drawing a picture showing yourself enjoying your favorite food:

Caring for the Body You Live In

In this activity, you can discover how a series of yoga poses helps you care for your mind and body. As you move through each pose, see if you can notice how the pose makes you feel, and appreciate how your body is able to move in different directions. You may want to use a yoga mat.

SUN POSE

Begin with Sun pose: Standing with your feet together, your legs straight, and your whole body standing strong, inhale and lift your arms out to the side and up toward the sky. Turn your head up to look at your hands and to say thank you to the sun for all of the ways it keeps you healthy and warm. As you exhale, look forward and bring your hands to your heart. You might thank your heart for being strong and nourishing your body with fresh oxygen in each breath. Repeat this Sun pose three times, inhaling and exhaling.

SUPERHERO POSE

Move into Superhero pose: Stand strong and tall with your hands on your hips and with your feet slightly apart, like a superhero would stand. Then, inhale and jump your feet apart, so your legs create a big triangle with the ground. Stretch your arms straight out to the side as high as your shoulders. Turn both feet to the right side. Don't forget to breathe! Bend your front leg to a right angle, keeping your back leg straight. Keep your arms straight. After one or two breaths, inhale and straighten your front leg and turn both feet forward, while placing your hands on your waist. See if you can feel the strength of your superhero. Now, repeat on the left side. Inhale and straighten the front leg after two or three breaths. Turn feet forward and jump them together to stand for three full breaths.

Move into Downward Dog pose: From a standing position, breathe in, and as you exhale, bend your knees and bring your hands to the floor. Step your feet back so that your body is making a large upside down V shape. Press your hands flat into the ground, straighten your legs, and don't forget to breathe. Breathe in and on the exhale, bend your knees so you can sit on your heels.

DOWNWARD DOG POSE

MORE

Move into Cat/Cow pose: Come to your hands and knees and spread your fingers wide. Check that your shoulders and elbows are directly over your hands and that your hips are directly over your knees. Make your back flat, like a tabletop. Inhale, and look up toward the ceiling and let your belly button drop toward the floor. Exhale, and gently drop your head and lift your belly button up toward your spine as you round your back. Repeat three to five times, moving your belly up and down as you breathe. To finish, inhale and make your back flat like a tabletop. Now, gently move onto your back and let your whole body rest quietly.

CAT POSE

COW POSE

End in Resting pose: With closed eyes and body in a relaxed position, focus on your breath for a few minutes. Quietly offer gratitude for your feet, legs, torso, arms, hands, heart, and head.

RESTING POSE

Now, circle the emoji or emojis that best show how you feel after this series of yoga poses.

"What I Like About Me" Penny Toss

It's a special thing to be a human being. How often do you stop to appreciate what you like about yourself as you are right now? This is a great way to help you grow gratitude in your brain and in your heart. You can create a game to help you practice this with a friend.

Materials you will need: markers or crayons, penny or small stone

Instructions:

1. Color and decorate the Penny Toss Game on the opposite page.

2. Lay the book open on the floor as flat as possible.

3. Step back three feet.

4. Gently toss your penny or stone onto one of the questions (close your eyes to make it harder!).

Take turns with a friend tossing the penny and answering the questions it lands on.

You can download this template at http://www.newharbinger.com/50645 and print it out.

How have you made it through a challenge?

WHAT IS YOUR FAVORITE THING ABOUT BEING A HUMAN?

WHAT ARE YOU HAPPY THAT YOU ARE OLD ENOUGH TO DO?

WHAT DO YOU HAVE FUN DOING?

WHAT DOES YOUR BODY LET YOU DO THAT YOU ENJOY?

What do you like about your age?

WHAT IS A SKILL YOU HAVE LEARNED?

How do you show people you care?

"Power of Positive Words" Poster

You may have heard that words can be very powerful! What words would you like to remember from this workbook as you come to the end of it?

Take a moment to create your own positive words poster on the opposite page to encourage you when you need it most. You might write out a loving-kindness wish for yourself. Or you might write out what you appreciate about yourself. You might even write what lesson or activity you want to remind yourself to practice from this workbook.

POWER OF POSITIVE WORDS

ACTIVITY 81

Congratulations!

You have now completed your workbook and are ready to take your mindfulness and self-compassion skills into the rest of your life. You have a lot of new tools that give you superpowers to help you manage any difficulty that comes your way.

So now you can write your name, using paints or markers, on your certificate at right.

You can also download the certificate template at http://www.newharbinger.com/50645 and print out to sign and decorate. Be sure to take some time to congratulate yourself for completing this workbook and building your toolkit.

 You can download this template at http://www.newharbinger.com/50645 and print it out.

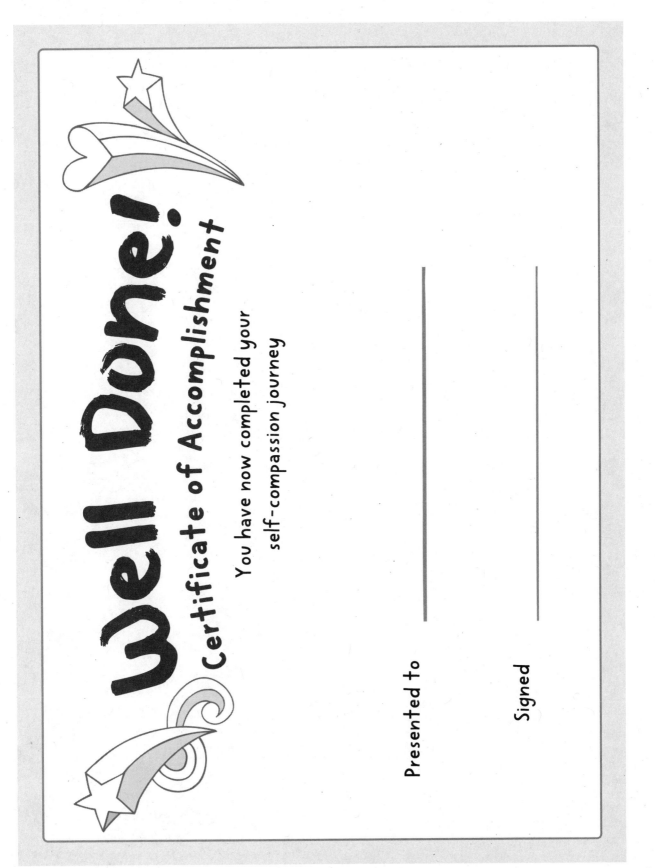

Well Done!

Certificate of Accomplishment

You have now completed your
self-compassion journey

Presented to _____

Signed _____

Building Your Toolkit

In this chapter, you've learned a lot of ways to show appreciation and gratitude. Remember you can always find something to be grateful for, which can be a big help when you are struggling.

Put a check mark next to the activities you learned in this chapter that you would like to try again:

___ Six Islands of Gratitude

___ Your Brain on Gratitude

___ "Thank You from Me to a Bee"

___ Gratitude Stick

___ "Thanks to the Many Hands that Feed Me"

___ Caring for the Body You Live In

___ "What I Like About Me" Penny Toss

___ "Power of Positive Words" Poster

___ Congratulations!

SHARING IS CARING

What gratitude practices would you like to share with a friend? Write a friend's name and the activity or idea that you would like to share.

Your friend's name: _____

What would you like to share with them? _____

_____

You now have a full toolkit to help you work with some of the challenges you might come across in your life! As you already know, things are not always so easy. But, if you practice what you've learned in this workbook, you will find that you have some great skills and even some superpowers that can make a difference in your life and in the lives of those you care about. Remember, sharing is caring!

Acknowledgments

This book is dedicated to all of the teachers whose pioneering spirit opened the door for kids around the world to become mindful and to learn to befriend themselves in challenging times. The wisdom and knowledge shared by these teachers will continue to influence and transform lives for many children and their families for generations to come. We are also grateful for the parents and children whose participation in the *A Friend in Me* curriculum helped to guide the creation of this workbook. We would also like to acknowledge the researchers who are committed to investigating the benefits of mindfulness and self-compassion as vehicles for stability and emotional regulation in kids and parents.

We are grateful to Drs. Kristin Neff and Chris Germer for their contributions and dedication to the field of self-compassion and without whom this workbook would not be available. Moreover, we would like to thank the Center for Mindful Self-Compassion and the University of California San Diego Center for Mindfulness for believing in this work and creating a pathway for teaching and developing material for the workbook. Finally, we would like to thank Tesilya Hanauer, Caleb Beckwith, and Vicraj Gill of New Harbinger Publications for the constant support and guidance offered throughout the creation of this workbook.

Lorraine: Years ago, when my husband John was still alive, we discussed the importance of bringing the teachings of mindfulness and self-compassion to children and families. He witnessed the subtle changes and the resilience brought forth in our own daughter. As Amy and I worked on the activities for the book, I often revisited our conversations, and his words gave me great comfort throughout. I know he would have been proud of us for bringing this fun-filled activity workbook to fruition. I also want to thank my daughter, Anna. She is a paragon of kindness and compassion in this world. Her sophisticated and wry humor often made its way into our working sessions. In addition, I would like to thank my dear friend and colleague Michelle Becker for her generous spirit and wise compassion. She was often a voice of reason. And, lastly, I would like to thank my coauthor, Amy Balentine, PhD. Her gentle nature and vast experience in working with kids and families in her psychotherapy practice added important dimensions to the creation of this workbook.

Amy: I would like to thank my husband, Scott, and our two teenagers who generously made space in our family life for the time needed to create this workbook and who also provided much needed technological support. I would also like to thank my friend Kim Erickson, a skilled editor and mindfulness practitioner, who offered valuable editorial feedback as we shaped the workbook. And I have the deepest gratitude for my mentor, Lorraine Hobbs, MA, who not only trained me in teaching mindfulness but graciously invited me to cocreate this workbook with her. Thank you for giving me this opportunity and collaborating with an open heart, a creative spirit, and an abiding enthusiasm for the project.

References

Germer, C., and K. Neff. 2018. *The Mindful Self-Compassion Workbook: A Proven Way to Accept Yourself, Build Inner Strength, and Thrive.* New York: Guilford Press.

Germer, C., and K. Neff. 2019. *Teaching the Mindful Self-Compassion Program: A Guide for Professionals.* New York: Guilford Press.

Neff, K. 2021. *Fierce Self-Compassion: How Women Can Speak Up, Claim Their Power and Thrive.* New York: HarperCollins.

Siegel, D., and T. Payne Bryson. 2012. *The Whole-Brain Child: 12 Revolutionary Strategies to Nurture Your Child's Developing Mind.* New York: Random House.

Lorraine M. Hobbs, MA, is founding director of the family and education programs at the University of California, San Diego (UCSD) Center for Mindfulness. Hobbs is cocreator of the mindful self-compassion for teens (MSC-T) program, and codeveloper of the MSC-T teacher training pathway. She is a certified teacher of mindful self-compassion (MSC), compassion cultivation training (CCT), and mindfulness-based stress reduction (MBSR). Hobbs is an MBSR mentor at the UCSD Mindfulness-Based Professional Training Institute. She is also codeveloper of A Friend in Me: Self-Compassion for Kids and Parents; and the Compassion in Parenting Program (CiP), adapted for parents of kids with autism spectrum disorder (ASD) and other neurodiverse challenges. Hobbs is coauthor of the book, *Teaching Self-Compassion to Teens*.

Amy C. Balentine, PhD, has practiced for more than twenty years as a clinical psychologist specializing in children and teens. She is founder and director of the Memphis Center for Mindful Living, LLC. She is also a qualified teacher of MBSR; and serves as a mindfulness teacher at the University of California, San Diego Center for Mindfulness; and also leads mindfulness classes and retreats for schools, nonprofits, and other organizations. Balentine is codeveloper of A Friend in Me: Self-Compassion for Kids and Parents.

Foreword writer **Kristin Neff, PhD**, is a pioneer in the field of self-compassion research, conducting the first empirical studies on self-compassion more than fifteen years ago. In addition to writing numerous academic articles and book chapters on the topic, she is author of *Self-Compassion*. In conjunction with her colleague, Christopher Germer, she developed an empirically supported, eight-week training program called Mindful Self-Compassion, and offers workshops on self-compassion worldwide.

MORE BOOKS from
NEW HARBINGER PUBLICATIONS

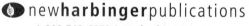
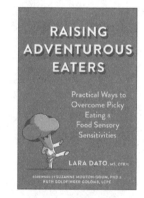